# Praise for dreams have no expiry date

"Although this book targets 'midlife' women, it can be picked up by any generation. It's so refreshing in its honesty, humor and humanity. And with few role models out there, it offers us real examples and guides to 'move forward, in any direction.' Go for it!"
—Ann Medina, broadcaster

"The authors of this book must have overheard every soul-searching conversation I've had with my women friends since our mid-forties. Their take on how best to live the last decades of our lives is both refreshing and inspiring. They are particularly attuned to women's unique ways of knowing and the importance of process, intuition and the ability to envision ways around obstacles rather than to think in terms of failure. There is value in this book for every woman who has ever pondered—and, I must say, every man as well."
—Marjorie Anderson, Ph.D., co-editor of *Dropped Threads* and *Dropped Threads 2*

"Insightful and inspirational, *Dreams Have No Expiry Date* is a must-read for those who are just beginning to dream or those who are building on their dreams. This self-help book wakes the reader up and encourages her to act. *Dreams Have No Expiry Date* is the perfect road map for a bright and ambitious woman of any age."
—Judith Shamian, RN, Ph.D, President and CEO, Victorian Order of Nurses (VON) Canada

"This book is a manual for living. It is a practical and inspirational guide on how to convert dreams into realities. It is great for women—or anyone—making transitions in life and work."
—Nancy Barry, President, Women's World Banking

# dreams

A PRACTICAL AND INSPIRATIONAL WAY

# have no

FOR WOMEN TO TAKE CHARGE OF THEIR FUTURES

# epiry

LAURIE GOTTLIEB, PhD, & DEANNA ROSENSWIG, MBA

# date

RANDOM HOUSE CANADA

www.randomhouse.ca

Library and Archives Canada Cataloguing in Publication

Gottlieb, Laurie Naomi, 1946–
Dreams have no expiry date : a practical and inspirational way for women to take charge of their futures / Laurie Gottlieb and Deanna Rosenswig.

ISBN 0-679-31290-0

1. Middle aged women—Conduct of life.  2. Self-perception in women.
3. Middle aged women—Attitudes.  4. Middle aged women—Interviews.
I. Rosenswig, Deanna  II. Title.

HQ1059.4.G67 2005      305.244'2      C2004-903411-1

Page 234 constitutes an extension of this copyright page.

Text Design: Kelly Hill

Photo of Laurie Gottlieb and Deanna Rosenswig:
Left of Centre Photography Services

This book is printed on paper that is ancient-forest friendly, 100% post-consumer recycled.

Printed and bound in Canada

10 9 8 7 6 5 4 3 2 1

*This book is dedicated to all Vantage Women who have come before us, journey with us and who will join and follow after us.*

# CONTENTS

# INTRODUCTION

WHAT WILL I DO WITH THE REST OF MY LIFE?

Rosalie wants to find a better balance in her life: *"The two things that have characterized my life have been ambition and rushing. I had to be the best. I had to do the best. And I had to rush to do as much as I could, as early as I could. I also had to be a great law professor, great mother, great wife, great home-maker—great at everything. I think that, having been influenced by the women's movement, we women in our forties have to do everything and we have to do it all well. We carry around this tremendous burden of having to be perfect—superwomen.*

*"I run my life like a Swiss train. Everything has to be on time because I have so many things going on. I'm starting to think that I've got to find a better balance in my life. It's not that I'm not happy. I am happy. I'm very grateful for what I have. But I feel that I am on a constant treadmill. 'What does everyone want for supper tonight?' as I'm running out the door. I sometimes just feel overwhelmed and I think there has got to*

*be a better way. I've got to find a way of striking a better balance. I just don't know how."*

Genevieve found herself suddenly unemployed. *"I've been a professional librarian for eight years. Before that I was an associate curator of a major book collection. I've just been laid off along with 30 percent of the staff. I'm fifty-eight years old and I decided that I would take this time to really reflect on what I want to do in terms of my career. I'm healthy and I don't see myself stopping work as long as it's stimulating. I've always been able to do work that I enjoy. I've never had a job that I didn't enjoy. But I am not sure what to do next."*

Sue was in her fifties, and a home-oriented mother of four, when her youngest child went away to university. She asked herself, What now? *"I was never interested in going out for lunch, shopping or playing bridge. During the years that I raised my children I filled my time by being involved in my children's school and in other community work. I just couldn't imagine how I would fill the void."*

Sibyelle found herself separated from her husband at the age of fifty-four, needing to work. *"I got married very young. I had children right away. I also did the wife thing. I did part-time work and had no education after high school. I didn't have the courage or the foresight to get a proper job while I was married. Nine years ago, after thirty-two years of marriage, my husband and I separated. It was extremely difficult for me. I am sixty-three now. I've really come into my own. I have three grown-up children and five grandchildren. I am encouraged by my children. I now work in an office. But I'm always worried about tomorrow. I am worried about what I will do if I lose my job."*

As a reader of this book, you are likely going through similar life changes. You have reached a period of your life when you've begun asking yourself, "What's next for me?"

The generation known as baby boomers, born between 1946 and 1964, are in, or about to enter, a new stage of their lives. This life stage is known as middle age or midlife. *Dreams Have No Expiry Date* is a guide for this stage of life and helps you to create a personalized road map to your future. *Dreams Have No Expiry Date* will help you to take charge of your life and create the future of your dreams.

Each woman arrives at this stage via a different route. In addition to the influences of biology and your personality, who you are at midlife is a function of the culture, political and social situations in which you have lived, the choices you have made, how you have coped with different situations and plain old luck. But middle-aged and older women remain the authors of their own life stories. There is still time to write some mighty good chapters.

You are a generation of women who defined for yourselves how you were going to live: married or single, straight or gay, as a parent or not, university educated or technically trained, work-oriented or home-centered. You are the same women who led your men into the labor and delivery rooms in the early 1970s and will now be leading with fresh ideas about work and leisure and how to get the most out of the rest of your life. *Dreams Have No Expiry Date* will help you look to and create a positive future.

The first thing to do is to banish the phrase *middle age* from your vocabulary. Middle age is associated with negative images of a life half over, the loss of youth, menopause, physical limitations, fewer work and life options. Call yourself middle-aged and you may think of your life as half over, which then limits your dreams.

We have coined the term *Vantage Years* to describe the ages between forty and sixty-five (and even beyond, for some women) because we believe they will prove to be years of advantage. Your wealth of experience and wisdom have positioned you at a new vantage point, giving you a clearer view on how you might create a meaningful future. Although there may be some contraction of work options at this stage in life, there is an expansion of options in other aspects of your life. The Vantage Years are your time to fulfill long-held dreams. We see this period as a time to build on your past and all that you have learned in years of living.

You've arrived at this time of life with the advantage of being a member of the boomer generation. Yours was the first generation to have benefited from higher education on a wide scale, better health care, the freedom afforded by birth control, job enrichment and the feminist revolution. Your generation will rewrite the way the world sees these later years. You boomers have never lived by the old rules. Why would you now?

Nicole told us that *"Fifty was a major turning point. I really believe that I truly became myself at fifty."*

Sally revealed that *"At this stage of my life, I would really like to do missionary work. I want to help the poor if I can and go and spend some time at Mother Teresa's convent in Calcutta. That's my dream. I have to do this. I'm able to achieve it now because my children are grown. I am a go-getter. This is what I have learned about myself."*

## How This Book Came About

We—Laurie and Deanna—have been friends since we met in Montreal at age twelve. Our friendship has survived moves, marriage, children, illnesses and different career paths. We attribute the longevity of our friendship to the fact that we love, respect and admire each other—and to the telephone.

Ever since Deanna moved from Montreal to Toronto thirty years ago, we have scheduled weekly telephone visits to catch up on events, bare our souls and share our dreams. We talk about everything: our children's progress, our diet and exercise programs (that aren't working), our relationship with our parents, illnesses and losses, our accomplishments and disappointments. We have talked at length about inner strengths and resources and about power. We have talked about recognizing, capitalizing on and mobilizing our potential and possibilities. We have been each other's sounding board, each looking to the other for support and advice. We have stood on the sidelines and applauded each other's successes. We have helped each other to succeed in the worlds of business and academia. And we have been struck by the similarities between these two worlds, even though the issues are clothed in different fabrics and follow different rules. Over thirty years of endless conversations, numerous issues have been discussed, countless problems have been solved. Despite hectic work and family schedules in various locations—Toronto, Montreal, London, New York, Chicago, Des Moines, Tokyo, Beijing, San Francisco—we have done our best to stay in touch.

During the course of one Saturday-afternoon chat between Toronto and Montreal, Deanna began describing some feelings and anxieties about her impending retirement from the bank where she had worked for more than thirty years. Deanna had risen to the level of Executive Vice President at the Bank of Montreal and had been a trailblazer in the financial field. She had been the first woman to serve as head of marketing, international banking and e-business at the bank, the first woman vice president of a major bank and one of the pioneers of Women's World Banking. And now she felt she was saying goodbye to that world.

The feelings and anxieties that Deanna was describing were familiar to Laurie, as she too was beginning to experience anxiety, but of a different nature. She was midway through a sabbatical year, having just completed six years as Director of the School of Nursing at McGill University, in Montreal. Laurie too was a trailblazer in her field. She was among the first nurses in Canada to earn a Ph.D. Her doctorate is in developmental psychology. She was one of the youngest directors of a hospital school of nursing in Canada, among the first to develop nursing programs in the college setting and the first Ph.D. program in nursing, as well as a pioneer nurse-scientist. She had decided to return to her role as professor rather than take another term as director, but she knew she would not be able to pick up where she had left off seven years before. The research world had changed; she had changed. She vacillated between apprehension and excitement about the future, self-doubt and confidence, uncertainty about the direction to take and yet a belief that all would become clear.

We recognized that the feelings and issues evoked by our impending life and work changes were part of a greater process of transition. What we realized that day on the phone was that if we were going through this process of change and feeling anxiety, surely other women must be experiencing the same. We decided to keep notes of our own experiences and feelings, and before we knew it, we had the beginnings of a book.

To mark the end of Laurie's term as Director of the School of Nursing, Deanna gave her a gift of a steel sculpture of a woman with her hands clasped together reaching for the sky. The sculpture was titled *Carpe Diem—Seize the Day!* Deanna had no doubt that Laurie's new adventure would take her to new heights. Laurie's gift to Deanna was a lapel pin of the four mothers in the Old Testament, Sarah, Rebecca, Leah and Rachel. These women, known for their strength, courage and wisdom, were productive and extremely accomplished in their middle years. Two gifts with two very poignant messages—even before this book was a twinkle in our eyes.

We had often shared a dream of working together and doing something for the betterment of women. Laurie had devoted her research to understanding caregiving (nursing, mothering, parenting) and early family development. Deanna has been a woman leader in banking and in microfinance. We believed we had something to offer women but we weren't quite sure what "it" might be. Besides, we were too caught up in our own families and our own work and our own lives to give the dream anything but a passing thought. Lucky for us, *Dreams Have No Expiry Date.*

## Why Do You Need This Book Now?

Today there are approximately seventy-six million North American baby boomers who are or will be reexamining their goals, resetting their priorities, and redefining themselves and their dreams. The oldest of the boomers are beginning to retire while the youngest of them are entering midlife. The youngest of the baby boomers turned forty in 2004.

Your challenges in this next phase of life will again be different from those of previous generations whose lives were delineated by more traditional roles. You will experience new challenges because the social landscape has radically changed and your futures are not clearly defined. More and more women, because of layoffs and early retirement, are finding themselves asking the question, "What am I going to do with the rest of my life?" at younger and younger ages. Others are facing life alone without a partner, either by circumstance or by choice. Others are looking to change paths in midstream, now that their children are grown, their mortgages paid off, and they have more freedom to make choices.

Articles appear weekly in newspapers and magazines focusing on career change, retirement blues and age bias. Many more articles report success stories about women who are living their dreams at more and more advanced ages:

- "And the winner is . . . the older woman" (Laura Holson, *The New York Times*, January 18, 2004)
- "The last hurdle for trail-blazing women: The gold watch" (Jane Gross, *The New York Times*, April 23, 2004)
- "Retired reborn: Canadians finding second acts for their lives" (Susan McClelland, *Maclean's*, March 2003)

- "Jane Pauley ready to take her next big step" (Peter Johnson, *USA Today*, May 6, 2003)

No doubt the number of articles and books on living the life you choose will increase exponentially in the coming years.

Those women who entered the workforce and who rose to positions previously reserved for men are facing rules of retirement and midlife written by men for men, based on men's needs and men's life-actuarial tables. Women have few role models to guide them through the process of transition and may have difficulty envisioning their life beyond forty-five. The paths that this generation of women will follow have not been traveled by previous generations of women.

This is a challenging time of life. Any challenge that requires a fundamental change in status, roles and relationships—such as when you go away to college, get married, become a mother, take a new job, move to a new city, get divorced or are widowed—requires some form of preparation. Preparation may not lessen the impact of the change, but it helps you cope better. Your generation is used to being prepared. You enrolled in premarital classes, prenatal classes and support groups, and you've flocked to therapists. You should also prepare yourself for this new phase in your life.

## This Book Is for You

This book is written for those women who live in the present, plan for the future and don't dwell on the past, no matter how illustrious or disappointing. If you have thought or can identify with one or more of the following statements, then this book is for you:

- I have been there, done that—I don't want to do this anymore.
- I have achieved my goals and need a new challenge. What's next? What are my choices?
- I need to find passion, new meaning and balance in my life.
- I had planned to retire at sixty-five but was retired fifteen years earlier.
- I want to do something just for me.
- I want to do something for others.
- Everything seems so uncertain all of a sudden; I'm questioning everything in my life.
- It's now or never.

If you are a career-oriented woman, a home-centered woman or someone who has combined working at home and working out of the home and are looking for change, this book is for you.

If you are a woman with dreams you'd like to realize, this book is for you.

If you are a woman contemplating retirement or worried about losing her job, this book is for you.

If you are a woman who has been recently divorced or widowed and need to redefine your life, this book is for you.

If you are any age and ready to take charge of your life, want greater independence and want to feel more in control, this book is for you.

## The Big Ideas in This Book

*Dreams Have No Expiry Date* will help you to take charge of your life and create the future of your dreams. Our goal is to show you how to get in touch with your dream and how to create a road map to make your dream your reality.

There are three major messages in this book:

- The best way to take charge of your future is to have a dream.
- It is never too late to create and achieve a dream because dreams have no expiry date.
- The Vantage Years are the ideal time of life to create and achieve dreams.

Dreams give life meaning and purpose. Everyone has a dream; some people just have difficulty identifying or articulating their dream. Some people think their dream is too insignificant to be considered a dream. Some people may even believe it is too late to dream. We believe you are never too old to dream. Women well into their eighties told us of their dreams. You *do* have a dream. You *can* be in charge. In Chapters 1 and 2 you will learn about dreams. In Chapter 3 you will identify your own dreams by completing a series of exercises.

Many women go through a process of transition during the Vantage Years. By reflecting on our own transitions and by listening to other women, we have identified five phases of this transitional process. We have named this process the Vantage Process. In Chapter 4, we describe it and its relevance to dreams and dreaming.

From years of learning and living, you have accumulated a lot of experience, wisdom and street smarts. It is these strengths that you will now call forth to help you take charge of your life. You will identify, assess and come to understand your strengths in Chapter 5. The next step, in Chapter 6, is to identify your resources in three basic areas: health, finance and relationships. These strengths and resources are what you will call on to realize your dreams.

Some ways of thinking about midlife are outdated and inappropriate yet prevail in the form of myths. You've probably heard the myth "You can't teach an old dog new tricks." These myths can become serious obstacles to dreaming. They can hijack dreams. These myths are described in Chapter 7 along with facts that debunk them.

In Chapter 8, you will assess how ready you are to move forward to fulfill your dream. This assessment will be based on how much you want the change and how seriously you intend to take action. As you proceed, you will understand just how motivated and ready you are.

Then in Chapter 9, you will create a personal road map to realize your dream. We give you the guiding rules of the road and activities to map out your own journey. You will also assess how close you are to realizing your dream by learning to read the signposts along the way. These signposts are outlined in Chapter 10.

In writing *Dreams Have No Expiry Date,* we have come to understand and appreciate the many challenges and successes that women weave together to create their own tapestry of a meaningful life. Throughout the book you will find stories and anecdotes about women who have created their dreams, the process they have gone through, what they have learned along the way and what they have found most helpful.

This book is not about rich women or famous women, although we have drawn inspiration from their stories. It is a book about women who are like all of us. In researching this book, we talked to more than one hundred women from different countries between the ages of forty and eighty-five who had made significant changes in the Vantage Years. We interviewed some of these women individually and others in small groups of four to eight. We held sessions in Montreal, Toronto, New York and London, England. These women shared their wildest dreams, deepest anxieties and the turning points in their lives. These are women with whom you can identify. We hope you will say, "If they can do it—so can I!"

But this book is more than a compilation of inspirational stories. We have looked for patterns in their experiences. By connecting the dots of these experiences, we have been able to paint a picture of what the Vantage Years have in store for you.

We tell women's stories to illustrate the challenges you will face in the Vantage Years. The simplicity of these stories and the fact that they may seem familiar should not mask the complexities with which you have to deal. Do not underestimate the challenge of this period in your life but do remember that you can get through it.

This book also contains guiding principles, tips and exercises. In some chapters there are exercises to complete. In other chapters we pose questions that you can ask yourself. These reflective questions are designed to get you thinking. Our experiences in business, in academia, in nursing and in life have taught us that change can best be achieved through active learning. You will get the most out of this book if you become actively involved in identifying your own dreams, understanding the Vantage Process, assessing your inner strengths, essential resources and readiness, and using what you have learned to guide you in creating your personal road map to your dream.

The decisions you make at this stage will profoundly affect how you live and experience the Vantage Years. You are the first generation of women who may live past ninety, in relatively good health. With thirty, forty or even fifty more years, you have half a lifetime ahead of you to dream and to realize your dreams. You are the first generation of women who can truly become the architects of your own lives and design your own future. And you are going to do it your way.

one

# DREAMS AND THE VANTAGE YEARS

WHEN LAURIE CELEBRATED HER fortieth birthday with her twin sister, Linda, it was at a special family celebration. Their children planned a party and selected the theme "Over the Hill"—three words imprinted on the invitations, napkins and a banner that was strung across the living room. The word *hill* was written on an imaginary cliff with the letters trailing off in a downward spiral. Everyone was amused by the children's choice of theme because they knew that the message simply didn't apply to the twins. In fact, quite the opposite. Linda and Laurie had not yet reached their peak. There were still many more hills to discover; many more hills to conquer.

At forty, you might laugh at this choice of theme because you don't believe that you are over the hill. At fifty, the joke no longer seems funny because you may feel there is an element of truth in this message; but even at sixty, seventy, eighty and beyond there is still more room for discovery.

During these Vantage Years, you will no doubt feel stirrings of unrest. These stirrings occur throughout your life but tend to be more acutely felt at midlife. They may be ill-defined and unarticulated, but they need to be attended to. They signal that the status quo is no longer working and that change is needed.

They may occur in women who look back with some measure of satisfaction that whatever they have done, they have done well. They may also occur in women who look back with some sense of disappointment at not having achieved what they had hoped. These stirrings can often be traced to as-yet-unarticulated dreams or dreams that have been articulated but have yet to be fulfilled.

Our message is simple: It is never too late to dream. Think of all the women whose lives took a new direction during the Vantage Years:

- Eleanor Roosevelt, at thirty-seven, became her husband's eyes and ears when Franklin D. Roosevelt, the future president of the United States, was felled by polio. Following her husband's death, Eleanor, who was sixty-one, increased her political activity significantly and became a powerful inspiration for the civil rights and women's movements.
- Katherine Graham, at forty-six, realized her dream of running the family business, the *Washington Post,* when she took over the helm following the suicide of her charismatic husband. Under her leadership, the *Washington Post* published the Pentagon Papers and exposed the Watergate debacle that led to the resignation of President Richard Nixon.

She also became an esteemed adviser to many
presidents.

- Dr. Ruth, in her fifties, launched her career as
  America's premier sex guru at a time when people
  assumed that when a woman her age goes to bed, she
  sleeps.
- Margot Fonteyn's ballet career was revitalized at forty-
  two when she partnered with Rudolph Nureyev, the
  famous Russian dancer.
- At fifty-two, Jean Paré, a Canadian housewife, turned a
  love for cooking into a multimillion-dollar enterprise
  with her *Company's Coming* self-published cookbook
  series.

As we said in the introduction, we have banished the
term *middle age,* with all its negative connotations and
messages, and relabeled this period of life the Vantage
Years. The Vantage Years, as the name suggests, reflects the
advantaged position in which you find yourselves now.
Because of your accumulated experience and wisdom you
are in a position to create and take full advantage of new
opportunities. You are now looking at your future from a
fresh vantage point with a clearer view of where you would
like to go.

Even if you arrive at these years believing you have
failed, been unsuccessful or have not lived up to your
promise, dreaming is possible. Some of you may have real
feelings of dread, despair or depression. You may feel down
on yourself because you think that life has passed you by.
You are exhausted by life's battles. We recognize that life
has been harder for some. But think of it this way: All the

problems and concerns you have already overcome have trained you well for what lies ahead. Everyone needs to have a dream. Even more so if you have had a difficult life. You still have half a lifetime to make changes and allow yourself to blossom.

Susan, now in her fifties, tells her story: *"My introduction into the working world really is a direct result of the sixties, because when I was sixteen I knew everything. I left home, got pregnant, gave up the baby, got busted for dope and realized that my parents knew a lot more than I thought they did. Then I went home, skipped grade twelve, went into grade thirteen and worked my way through university."* Susan's life has taken many twists and turns, but since her rocky start, she has made major contributions to the fields of health care, education and business.

Some of you are facing a multitude of new problems and concerns such as menopause, ailing parents, misdirected children, illness, straying husbands, unrequited love, ageism in the workplace. These challenges sap your energy and dominate your life, making it harder to recognize the positives and possibilities that are hiding everywhere.

What we are here to tell you is that the Vantage Years are the ideal time for you to create opportunities that are challenging, satisfying and rewarding. Now is the best time to discover unique, untapped strengths and resources and find new direction. Now is the time for you to get in touch with your dreams. There is no better age in a woman's life than the Vantage Years to live her dreams.

In this chapter you will learn the answers to these questions:

- What are dreams?
- Why don't dreams have an expiry date?
- Are dreams different at different ages and different stages in the life cycle?
- Why are the Vantage Years the ideal time for realizing dreams?

## What Are Dreams?

What comes to your mind when you hear the word *dream?* Words like *need, desire, goal, task, striving, aspiration, mission* and even a *calling* are aspects of what you might call dreams.

A dream is something that is hoped for, wished for or longed after. Dreams speak to a bright future, even when the present is fraught with anxiety and stress.

When we interviewed women about their dreams and how they defined the word *dream,* each had a different understanding of the meaning. Andrea, an architect, explained: *"Dreams are way out there—more elusive than goals, less definable than goals—larger than life."* For some, dreams are fantasies or daydreams, the unattainable or never-to-be realized hope.

In our book, dreams are attainable. They are more possible than fantasy and broader than a goal. We deliberately use the word *dreams* rather than *goals* or *aspirations* because dreams speak to your vision of who you are and what you might do. We prefer the word *dream* because it allows you to be more expansive and open to imagination and invention. The broader your definition, the greater the possibilities of expression. For example, a goal might be to become vice-president of your company, but a dream might be to become a leader. The dream can be expressed in a variety of ways: in your job, through participation on boards, or even through political leadership or community leadership.

Linda, who had a business designing sweaters and now owns a business designing beautiful cakes, summarized her quest to realize her dream to be creative: *"I wasn't happy with myself because I felt I wasn't being productive. I wanted to do something creative but I didn't know what to do. I tried a couple of things. They were all artistic. I don't consider myself an artist at all, but I can learn anything. So I tried furniture painting and I tried making pillows from antique fabric with my old sewing machine. And none of those things really did it for me. At the same time I was taking other kinds of courses—academic courses. I was keeping busy, but I wasn't happy. When I designed sweaters, I was in business at a time when few women in their thirties and forties had businesses. But when I started designing and decorating cakes, I really felt that, artistically, I came into my own."*

Monette, an entrepreneur, told us that after working for many different organizations, her dream was never to work for someone else again. *"I was only going to work for me, no matter what, so that I could be in control."* The dream of being her own boss propelled her into her current career. *"I now have my own insurance brokerage firm. I am in charge."*

Put the idea of *fantasy* behind you. Think of dreams in a new way. Dreams are real; they are not fantasy. They are only unreal until you, the dreamer, articulate the dream, label the dream, validate the dream and then make plans to implement the dream.

You may still be having the following dialogue with yourself: "The idea of having a dream is foreign to me. It's not the way I think or talk about my future. In fact, if someone were to ask me, 'What is your dream?,' I would not have an answer. And if I were forced to answer, I would have to invent a dream." You may really believe that you do not have a dream. But everyone has dreams. Dreams are within you, waiting to be discovered.

If you really still can't relate to the word *dreams,* find a term with which you are more comfortable. Express what you want for your life in words that make sense to you. If words like *life-goal, life-striving, mission* and *direction* work better for you, then use them.

Now that you have an appreciation of what dreams are, we are going to find out why dreams do not have an expiry date.

## Why Don't Dreams Have an Expiry Date?

Lettie, in her seventies, tells of her odyssey to realize her dream of becoming an Anglican priest. *"My story is almost backwards because I made the decision when I was sixteen years old to become an Anglican priest, but I was not allowed to do what I wanted to do. I shouldn't say I made the decision. At sixteen I felt called to be an Anglican priest. That was in England and of course anywhere in the world you couldn't be a woman Anglican priest. I did my service in the air force and then applied to Cambridge University and I sent in my transcript and just signed L. James. I was invited in for an interview and oh my God! Archbishop Ramsey, as he eventually became, was the dean of theology and I went in and he said, 'It's a woman!' I said, 'Yes, sir,' just to confirm it. He decided no. There was no way I would be admitted to theology school. And I fought and fought and fought and eventually was admitted to St. John's. But I had to live at St. Hills, which was the women's college. And there were over three hundred male students and one woman. I graduated. The men went on to be ordained and of course, I couldn't. I stayed and did my master's. I stayed and did my doctorate. I thought, 'Surely someone will employ me,' but nobody would employ a woman to teach theology in England. So I went to King's College in London and did my doctorate in clinical psychology, really thinking that in that way I was doing a lot of the things I would be doing as a priest. Then in 1951, I got married and we came to Canada and, of course, found the same obstacle. I did some counseling. Then my husband was in the space program and we moved to Atlanta. I got a job teaching theology at Emory University. At least they were a wee bit more progressive. In 1971, we came back to Montreal, and of course the same thing happened. Women clergy were anathema in the Anglican Church, except there were a number of priests who would invite me to preach or to counsel. So, really I had the run of the diocese in many ways. In 1974, at our general synod, which is the meeting of all the church representatives, they decided that in every parish and every diocese the issue of the ordination of women to the priesthood would be discussed. Eventually they decided that women could be ordained in*

*principle. Of course, I wrote and told them that women existed
in reality. Anyway, I went to my bishop who was a very shy and
good man but really not able to make any decisions that went
against the flow of what people wanted. He said, 'You're
already trained.' He hemmed and hawed. Eventually, in 1976 he
ordained me to the deaconate. You usually become a deacon for
a year and then a priest. But the two men who were ordained
with me were made priests a year later but I wasn't. I hung on
and hung on until Lambert—at the meeting of the bishops from
all over the world—decided that a woman could be ordained. In
1978, I was ordained as a priest—the first in the diocese of
Montreal. That was a great occasion. There was a great organized protest from across the country. Yesterday, I was reminded of
an interview I did in 1976 when the archbishop said, 'There is
no more possibility in ordaining a woman than there is ordaining a monkey.' I had forgotten about that. How could I?"*

Another dream whose flame was kept alive was
Beverly's. A retired college teacher, just shy of her sixtieth
birthday, told us, *"I dreamt of having a vineyard. This was my
dream for over thirty years. I have just planted the first plant.
It's a small dream but I finally made it a reality. I am thrilled."*

You have grown up at a time when many products have
an expiry date and the idea of an expiry date is ingrained in
your psyche. You may throw out a carton of milk based on
the expiry date rather than on the smell. This notion, sadly,
permeates other areas of our lives. It is hazardous for your
health if you believe that expiry dates pertain to you: "it's too
late," "past your prime," "gone bad," "used up," "no good."
This book will show you that age is not a major determinant
of what you can and cannot achieve. Don't accept someone
else's notion of expired, ended and over.

Many women sense a disconnect between their chronological age and how they feel inside. We often hear women say, "I know the number is fifty-three but I feel the same as I did when I was twenty-five, in my heart and in my head." And they might add, "I still have lots of things happening in my life. I'm looking forward to my next adventure." Expiry dates may apply to products; they do not apply to dreams or aspirations.

Some sectors of society have imposed a "best-before" date through a mandatory retirement age that does not take into account a person's abilities or desires. Athletes and dancers have short peak-performance years and live under the cloud of a "best-before" date. Those who extend the date tend to be the exception, but there are wonderful exceptions from which to learn. Consider Martha Graham, a modern dancer and choreographer who led her own company and performed well into her seventies. Mick Jagger of the Rolling Stones still draws crowds at age sixty. Shannon Lucid, in her mid-fifties, who is a grandmother and American astronaut, has been on the MIR space station longer than any other woman. Reaching new heights as they matured, all these people have performed in their chosen fields past normal retirement dates.

In other sectors where knowledge, wisdom and experience are valued, a premium is given to people over forty. Think of the average age of our politicians, the volunteers in nonprofit organizations, academics, company directors, physicians. As Faith, a university professor, told us: *"At the university we don't experience ageism because most tenured professors are middle aged. The younger colleagues are lower in the pecking order . . . they're not tenured yet, they haven't established themselves the way we have. Especially in the humanities and social sciences—my field—you just get better as you get older—like old wine. I have invested fifteen years of my life in becoming extraordinarily specialized in one particular field of scholarship."*

Humans are by nature goal-directed and as such are programmed from birth with capacities to explore, and to develop new skills and interests—capacities that last for life. You never outgrow or become too old for dreaming.

If you need further persuasion, stop and look around. Older people still buy lottery tickets and plan for their future. At eighty-two, Martha goes to the office every day with her eighty-four-year-old husband. They run their business and are planning their next vacation. At eighty-six, Evelyn S. continues to be a social activist, taking part in public protests about the health-care system. She is trying to organize a group to help new immigrant women improve their English. In their eighties, Rose and Gertrude found new part-time jobs as extras in movies. Emily is ninety-two and got angry when the insurance company wouldn't sell her a five-year extended warranty on her new car. These women have dreams and are still dreaming.

Katherine, in her forties, began a company that organizes corporate events, meetings and conferences in Canada, the United States and Europe. *"At forty I started my own company. I had to do that because I was totally unemployable. I was a forty-year-old married woman who hadn't worked in sixteen years. I had a degree in art history but had many other interests. I came up with three business ideas that would fit into my life because I had children and I wanted to be able to be available to them."*

Pat, living in England, first went to university at fifty-three to fulfill a lifelong dream of getting a university education. *"My children had always come first. Several years ago, I decided to train as a lay reader in the church. I settled into the ministry but I always felt that the academic side was missing. I moaned about this constantly. I felt terrible—inadequate, defensive about my lack of formal education. About three years ago, when my youngest was old enough and my husband had retired, I began taking courses in Christian studies."* Pat is now working on a master's degree.

Sandra and John were in their twenties when they fell in love with France. When John retired from being a university professor, forty years later, they figured out a way to buy an apartment in Paris to realize their dream of spending winters there.

Michaela, an investment banker and founding president of Women's World Banking in New York, had always been an advocate for and mentor of young women. After she retired in her sixties she took on consulting work and also began teaching a course in women's leadership at a New York college.

Each of you knows someone who didn't give up on her dreams, because dreams have no expiry date!

## Are Dreams Different at Different Ages and Different Stages in the Life Cycle?

Your dreams reflect the developmental tasks that are paramount at any given stage of your life and so they will change throughout your lifetime. During the young-adult years, dreams revolve around yourself, finding a partner and establishing intimacy, a career, raising a family and seeing the world. During the middle-adult years, dreams often shift to the need for more meaningful involvement in and integration of work and personal life. Gail Sheehy's book *New Passages* drove this point home when she labeled each of these decades to capture their central theme: the "Flourishing Forties," the "Flaming Fifties," the "Serene Sixties," the "Sage Seventies," the "Uninhibited Eighties," the "Noble Nineties," the "Celebratory Centenarians."[1]

Even within the Vantage Years people dream different dreams of health, wealth, relationships, achievement, meaning and purpose in life. Notwithstanding the central theme within each decade, dreams are complex and there is wide individual variation. Your dreams during these adult years are affected by myriad factors including not only your age but also your attitude, your life circumstances, the culture in which you live, your health, the health of your parents and other family members, the age of your children, your financial situation and so on.

Another major factor affecting who you are in this period of life is the year in which you were born. Women who are now in their late fifties and sixties were married and had children in their twenties, whereas women in their early fifties may not have had children until they were well into their thirties. Forty-year-old women may be just contemplating marriage and children now. Seventy-year-old women rarely worked outside the home. The women who will be seventy years old in ten or twenty years are currently working outside the home. We all arrive at the Vantage Years having taken multiple and varied pathways.[2] The person you married, or if you partnered at all, the different bends in your road, your major turning points, deaths, accidents, personal circumstances, your decisions—have all made you the person you are today.

Heather's story is definitely more a reflection of what is going on in her life than her chronological age. *"I turned fifty this year. I've been thirty years in nursing across several provinces and have been seventeen years in a senior leadership position in one institution. I'm out of sync because I've been married for twenty-two years but I have a thirteen-year-old daughter. I'm not talking about her marriage for at least ten years and I may not be having grandchildren until I'm seventy. I was married for ten years before we had our first child. I feel as though I'm totally out of step with other fifty-year-olds. I was too young for Woodstock and now I am not ready for retirement."*

It is not surprising that desires, priorities and interests shift and change over time. Dreams, once fulfilled, need to be replaced. Some dreams may become irrelevant or even redundant. At forty, you may be looking for a better job and more money. At fifty, you may not be at the stage in your career you had wanted or expected to be. On the other hand, you may have surpassed your wildest expectations. At sixty, you may be looking for new meaning in your life and a chance "to give back" or to have more time for yourself.

The Vantage Years are a period of reflection and reevaluation. Some women have told us that they no longer need to be ahead of the curve. The woman who thought she would make partner or be president and didn't achieve these goals may decide that she didn't want to be president, given the sacrifices required, or she may accept that becoming president will not happen. That acceptance is healthy. Some women come to this point in their lives and realize they will never achieve what they had dreamt for themselves. They need to come to terms with this disappointment before they can move on. This acceptance is liberating and helps them dream different dreams. Many women are planning for retirement at this stage while others want to delve deeper into their chosen area. Faith also told us: *"When I'm thinking of transitions in my life, right now I'm not thinking at all about changing my job. Quite the contrary. I'd like to dig deeper into my job."*

Some of the women we interviewed confided that, as they moved into their fifties, they questioned what they were doing with their lives. Angie described the debate she was having with herself about her future: *"I'm in transition. I left the company I was with. What I find interesting right now is that a lot of people told me, 'When you get into your late forties, early fifties, you're going to see things differently. You're going to probably want to do different things.' I never believed that. I thought I wanted to keep climbing up the corporate ladder. I wanted to get to the top—whatever the top was. Now I have an opportunity to get back into the corporate world in a bigger job, bigger bucks and bigger everything. And now I'm thinking, 'I don't know if I want to do that.' I found it interesting that when you get to forty-seven you're not thinking about your career in the same way anymore. Do I really want to work fourteen hours a day? Do I really want to be totally focused on a corporation or do I want to be more involved at the university? Do I want to do more things in the community? My family? Or do I want to get back into the rat race?"*

Another recurring theme that Vantage women talked about was the fear of regrets. Women we interviewed talked about regret over *not* having done something rather than regret over having done something. Alta best summed up the thoughts of others when she said, *"I don't want to look back when I am old and sick and say, 'Why didn't I?'"*

## Why Are the Vantage Years the Ideal Time for Realizing Dreams?

Faith says, *"I think one of the most interesting things about getting older is that I associate it with getting dreamier, getting less focused. To be a scholar is to become a certain kind of person. You have to follow where your mind is taking you. At this point in my life, I arrived at the stage where I have accomplished certain things. My interests are fanning out in totally bizarre directions. Whatever I thought I knew, I now don't know any longer or don't want to know any longer. I am finding this totally delightful."*

This is the ideal time for dreaming

- because of your knowledge and life experiences.
- because of your strengths.
- because of the period in which you have lived.
- because you have fulfilled your obligations to others.
- because you have the time.
- because of new freedoms.
- because you are more aware of the passage of time.

**Because of your knowledge and life experiences.** You come to this age with a wealth of knowledge, wisdom and street smarts gained from learning and living. You have a deeper understanding of yourself, greater self-acceptance, and you have learned how to manage your basic disposition or personality. With effort, you are better at controlling your temper, are more tolerant and less critical of your own messy ways or your tendency to procrastinate. You may also find you are less sensitive to the criticism of others. *"This is liberating,"* Odette explained, *"I know who I am. I'm not afraid. I know my weaknesses and if others don't like me, they don't like me. It's too bad. It is so wonderful to be free of caring about the opinions of others."*

**Because of your strengths.** No matter where you are in your life or how you have come to the Vantage Years, you have come through many trials. In the process, you developed a wide range of creating, coping and connecting skills that will enable you to realize your dreams. Leading up to the Vantage Years, you have developed many areas of knowledge and life skills, one at a time, often stored in separate silos. During the Vantage Years you can bring these skills together, into a new integrated whole.

**Because of the period in which you have lived.** Your birth year and the period of history in which you have lived have had a hand in shaping who you are today.[3] Born after the Second World War into a future of unprecedented prosperity, the boomer generation was brought up to believe in themselves and that anything was possible. For many, this was a time of euphoria, optimism, growth and prosperity. Influenced by the feminist movement, this generation redefined societal rules for work and family for both men and women and created a new social order. The boomer generation was brought up during a time when nutritious food and good health care were readily available. While we are mindful that this was not everybody's experience, many of you are leading far healthier lifestyles than your parents, and understand the benefits of good nutrition, exercise and the importance of moderating stress. You are facing forty and perhaps fifty years more of life.

**Because you have fulfilled your obligations to others.** During the earlier adult years, women tend to suppress their own interests and place the needs of their children, family and career first. You all know women who stayed in a job they didn't like because their families depended on their income, or women who interrupted their careers to care for children and parents. You yourself might not have been able to realize your dreams because you lacked the emotional or financial resources or because responsibilities intervened. Daniel J. Levinson, a pioneer scientist in midlife adult development, explained the BOOW notion: Becoming One's Own Woman as a critical driver in signaling middle age.[4] By this time in your life, you are not as central in your children's lives and are ready to do something for yourself.

**Because you have the time.** During this period of your life, you have more time to do what you want to do. Evelyn B. told us: *"In my forties, I was overscheduled. In my fifties, life was less fettered, less hectic. This was the beginning of my time to realize my dream of travel with my husband."* Katherine is relishing the time for herself: *"I was always afraid of this stage of my life. What's going to happen when my kids aren't around anymore, when it's just me and my husband? Is our relationship going to change? I love this stage of* *my life. I was telling my husband last week, 'I have more time now to do things that I couldn't do before.'"*

**Because of new freedoms.** Having freedom is more than just having time. Freedom means that you can do what you want, when you want and how you want. Freedom often means giving yourself permission to do what you want and to give priority to your dreams. Monette says: *"I find that between the ages of forty-five and sixty-five, women are blossoming—coming into their own. They are turning around and saying, 'I have a world in front of me. My children are gone now. I don't have to take care of them. My husband is doing his thing. I'm doing my thing. But my own time now is for me.' I see them doing incredible things at this age. I've seen these incredible women who say, 'I've got all this power in front of me. I now have power because I am now able to spend a lot more energy on me and where I want to go and what I want to do.'"*

**Because you are more aware of the passage of time.** Dreams may look very different during the Vantage Years because of your increasing awareness of time passing and your heightened sense of urgency to begin to act on your dreams. You are probably finding yourself becoming more aware of how you spend and allocate your time. You are likely to be less patient with things that seem like a waste of time. If you have an ambition or desire to do something, the Vantage Years are not the time to procrastinate. Avra verbalized what many women are thinking: *"My biggest fear is running out of time. When you are young you say, 'I will do it when I am older' and now I am older."*

As they confront close friends' illnesses and early deaths, many women report that they are increasingly aware of their own mortality. Rosalie expressed these sentiments: *"Now that I am in my forties, I realize I don't have that much time left. My life is half over. God willing, it's not more than half over. After all, not everyone makes it to eighty. I knew a woman in her fifties who just died from a brain tumor. It's this pull between realizing that we don't have all that time left so we've got to enjoy the time we have, but on the other hand, we still have to work very hard. When you're in your twenties and thirties you have your whole life ahead of you—if you don't do it this weekend, you'll do it next weekend. That's the real difference between your twenties and forties—you become aware of your own mortality."*

## Women, Take Charge of Your Life!

The Vantage Years give you a second chance to reclaim or redeem aspects of yourself that may have lain dormant for many years. Nicole shared the dream of her youth and how this dream has never left her. *"Making a difference was one of my dreams. I used to joke when I was very young, when things weren't going well, I would say, 'Je pars pour le Gabon—I am going to be a missionary in Gabon.' It's still in the back of my mind somewhere. I may end up in a very strange place one day doing—I don't know what. But I've left the doors open. My luxury now that I'm a freelancer is to be able to say no. I don't have to do anything I don't want to do. I don't have any constraints. That's an incredible luxury. Until I was fifty, I spent my life running around, trying to make things happen. Trying to fix things that didn't work. Trying to recover from this. Trying to reach that . . ."*

Because the Vantage Years are ideal for dreaming, you now need to take charge of your life in order to create and take advantage of opportunities. To take charge of your life you need to know where you are going and create a plan to get there. To take charge, you have to focus on moving forward. To take charge, you must call on all your strengths and resources to make bold moves.

Taking charge may seem daunting. But it needn't be, because being in charge means just that—you are the boss, the one calling the shots.

You can control

- the scope of the task.
- the speed of implementation.
- the way you call forth and develop your strengths and resources.
- the size of the steps you decide to take.

There is a big world out there over which you may have limited control. But what you can control is your own reaction to the world. You have faced many turning points in your life and you have taken charge, even in the smallest ways. Charlotte told us about her turning point: *"At forty I went back to work, got a divorce, learned to drive."* Her metaphor for taking charge was learning to drive.

The rest of this book is devoted to helping you find the right vehicle and climb into the driver's seat.

two

# WHY YOU NEED TO HAVE DREAMS

SANDY'S LIFE HAS REVOLVED around her husband, three children and seven grandchildren. She was engaged at eighteen, married at nineteen and has been happily married for almost forty years. She worked as an elementary school teacher and a real estate administrator. It was in her fifties that she found the way to really express her dream when she embarked on a five-city tour as a stand-up comedian.

She describes her younger self as a shy girl. Her husband, with a twinkle in his eye, recalls bringing Sandy home and having his mother ask him, "Does she speak?" Speak she does! This highly articulate, vivacious woman has captivated audiences across the country with her piercing observations of married life.

The seeds for Sandy's career were sown more than twenty years ago when she took her daughter to audition for a play and they both ended up joining the troupe. Sandy tells how when she donned the wig, words magically came out of her mouth. People were stunned at Sandy's transformation from an elegant, quiet woman to a beautiful, raucous, audacious whore, all with the help of a costume and a red wig.

Sandy continued acting for years and found she needed the props to get into character. She needed the lines someone else had written to give her a voice. Then, one day, she found herself on a stage—no props, no lines—just Sandy . . . and a stand-up comedian was born. She found her voice and a new passion in her fifties. Sandy loves people. She loves sharing her observations and perceptions of the world with them. She loves entertaining them and bringing happiness. She enjoys the magic of the stage as well as the applause and recognition. When asked why she did it, she simply answered: *"I don't want to come to the end of my life and have regrets about what I was too afraid to do."*

Sandy is living her dream because her dream speaks to her spirit, her hopes and longings. Her dream was broad enough to find expression in different forms at different stages in her life. Her dream has added texture to an already full life.

In this chapter you will learn the answers to these questions:

- What are the characteristics of dreams?
- Why are dreams necessary?
- What are the prerequisites for dreaming?
- What are the obstacles to dreaming?

## What Are the Characteristics of Dreams?

As you learned in Chapter 1, a dream is a vision that is larger than a goal and more achievable than a fantasy or an aspiration. A dream can range from something circumscribed or small to something grand. A dream can be experienced in varying degrees of intensity from "I must be," "I must have," "I must do," through to "I really want to," "I might want to," "I am inclined towards."

Regardless of whether your dream is small or large, an authentic dream must

- be meaningful to you.
- be consistent with your values.
- resonate with who you are and how you see yourself.
- be owned by you.
- give you a direction for your future and occupy a significant place in your life.
- be motivated by interest and curiosity.
- be realistic or within the realm of possibility.
- be accompanied by a feeling of fulfillment and satisfaction.
- bring you joy.

**A dream must be meaningful to you.** Genevieve has a passion for gardening. *"I belong to a community garden and I used to have a friend with whom I gardened for many years . . . So this week I went to the botanical gardens for an information session about their two-year horticulture program. The idea of learning all the Latin names of flowers is wonderful . . .*

*I'm thinking that gardening is something I can continue until I'm a very ripe old age."* If a dream is meaningful, you will be motivated to act.

**A dream must be consistent with your values.** Joyce said, *"I was raised to get married and have children. Go to university, but get married, have children and stay at home with your children. It never entered my head that I would be doing anything other than raising children. I loved being a mother; I still do. When we were younger, my husband started his own business. As soon as the children were old enough to go to school I used to work three days a week but I took them to school every morning and picked them up every afternoon. And that's how I worked it out. I worked with my husband and right away he said we were business partners. We have been married over thirty years. We could have just as easily grown apart as together. I feel very lucky . . . it's more than lucky, but I'll use the word lucky right now. I always dreamt of caring for my family. I am a caregiver for my family. If someone dear to me, and even some who aren't dear to me, are in need, I am the one who takes care of people."* If a person's dream does not accurately represent their ideals and values it will undermine their sense of well-being because the emotional cost of pursuing the wrong dream will be too high.

**A dream must resonate with who you are and how you see yourself.** Fatima, a doctor by training, decided at forty to leave medicine to pursue her passion of singing professionally. As she told us, *"I wanted to follow my essence."*

What you have done all your life may not be what you have to do for the rest of your life. This is the time to get in touch with those interests that have been limited by work and to find interests that add new dimensions to your life. When there is a good match between your dream, what you value and who you are, chances are you are going to feel passionate about your dream.

**A dream must be owned by you.** Terri realized after being in dental practice for several years that dentistry was not her dream but that of her parents. She left dentistry to renovate old houses. She enjoys the work and likes herself better. Many of you may feel you have come to these years having lived someone else's dream. With the passing of time, the time to reflect and maybe even the benefit of therapy, you are ready to live your own life.

**A dream must give you a direction for your future and occupy a significant place in your life.** Nancy's dream has always been to help poor women gain financial access to their local economies. She is the leader of Women's World Banking, a network of organizations that provides financial services to over fifteen million low-income entrepreneurs, primarily women, in more than forty countries. In achieving and living her dream for more than twenty years, Nancy has touched the lives of millions of people. Dreams can set you on a course or path for a significant number of years and can take up a significant portion of your time and energy.

**A dream must be motivated by interest and curiosity.** Sylvia and her husband, both physicians, became curious about how the medical profession approached professional behavior in medicine. They got hooked on the subject during their sabbatical year when they were both in their sixties. Sylvia's interest was sparked by doctor strikes and her husband's by the government assuming more control over the medical profession. As Sylvia explained, *"We got absolutely intrigued by professionalism in medicine . . . You get intrigued by something and find it's terrific. And then on you go. And we got intrigued because the literature was there."* Dreams must be twigged by curiosity and sustained by interest.

**A dream must be realistic or within the realm of possibility.** Alta told us about her dream. *"I decided that when I retired I would embark on my lifelong dream of learning Italian. It seemed like an exciting project. Much to my surprise it was not as easy as I had anticipated. Having taught Latin close to forty years ago and knowing French as well, I was certain that I would take to Italian in a snap. Well . . . my ability to absorb a new language at this stage in my life was not so easy. However, I am persevering. I attend an Italian class once a week and thoroughly enjoy this activity. My classmates are in the same frame of mind as I am, so we laugh a good deal and forge on! All in all, it is a challenging experience which I love. My retirement days are truly fun. How blessed I am."* The more realistic and attainable the dream, the greater the chance of realizing it.

**A dream must be accompanied by a feeling of fulfillment and satisfaction.** Letha, a past chairperson of the Board of Wellspring, which runs centers that support cancer patients and their families, explains her passion for this work: *"This is where my real passion is and it's because it has been fun to be part of something unique and very entrepreneurial. We have five centers now and several more are planned across Canada. This work has been the real highlight of my volunteer career."*

**A dream must bring you joy.** Naomi gave up a senior position in a major corporation and is devoting time to her children and grandchildren. *"I've enjoyed the last two and a half years. I like where I'm at. Retirement to me is liberation and freedom."*

The ultimate dream is one that makes your heart soar and your adrenaline rush. Dianne confides: *"I was lying in bed and I imagined my future career as a philanthropy consultant. I felt the same rush of excitement as I had felt when I went off to college for the first time. It was the same feelings of excited anticipation—not knowing what lay ahead but knowing it would be wonderful."*

## Why Are Dreams Necessary?

As Alice made her way through Wonderland she met the Cheshire cat and asked for directions: "Would you tell me, please, which way I ought to go from here?" "That depends a good deal on where you want to get to," said the cat.[1]

Dreams are necessary because they

- give life purpose, direction and meaning.
- shape lifestyle choices.
- focus you on the future and give you a sense of control.
- fill you with hope.

- are an expression of your potential and give voice to that potential.
- are a source of pleasure.

**Dreams give life purpose, direction and meaning.** The cat knew something that Alice was about to learn—unless you know where you are going, you won't know when you have gotten there. No matter how vague or amorphous your dream seems, it points you in a direction.

Without a dream where do you go? Denise moves steadily in the direction of her dream of helping people who are vulnerable. *"I always was fascinated by health care. I was always fascinated by caring—being with people, helping people. I was very attracted by the sciences, biology. When I became a community health nurse, my idea was to become an advocate for people. And that's what I did for quite a while with different kinds of people—people who were new immigrants. I was working in a very poor neighborhood. Poverty was the main trigger for me. My doctoral thesis examines the frail elderly, the kind of care we give them and how nurses advocate for care when the elderly have to go from one organization to the other. Nurses make the bridge. So that's always been an interest of mine."* Research shows that people with purpose report a greater sense of well-being and are happier and more satisfied.[2]

**Dreams shape lifestyle choices.** If your dream is to make money, the choices you make about work will be very different than if your dream is to have lots of free time for your family. If making money is your dream, you will seek higher-paying positions or professions, which may be more time-consuming. If having lots of free time with your family is your dream, you may choose to work part-time or at a less demanding job.

**Dreams focus you on the future and give you a sense of control.** Many people feel frightened about the future. What frightens them is the uncertainty, the unpredictability of not knowing what will happen. People would worry less about the future if they had a sense that they could create it. Dreams allow you to create that future.

**Dreams fill you with hope.** Dreams are about making things better and brighter. A dream shows you what you can look forward to. Barbara, an entrepreneur, tells us: *"Dreams are important because they give you hope. How can you continue to live without dreams?"* Hope is a great motivator to action. Christopher Reeve, the actor who played Superman and who was paralyzed from a spinal cord injury, dreamt of walking again. His dream will live on in the Christopher Reeve Paralysis Foundation, which, even after his death in 2004, continues to search for a cure for paralysis and so gives hope to others.

**Dreams are an expression of your potential and give voice to that potential.** All of us have some unexplored interests or talents. By exploring those talents, you are being true to yourself. You need to articulate your dream to give yourself a chance. There are dreams inside each of us. Think of the many people who picked up a paintbrush and easel in their Vantage Years and discovered their own distinctive style of expression.

**Dreams are a source of pleasure.** Many people buy a lottery ticket and derive great joy dreaming about how they will spend the winnings, knowing full well what the odds are. The price of the ticket buys hours of dreaming.

## What Are the Prerequisites for Dreaming?

Everyone has a dream. To get in touch with your dream, you need to create the best conditions to make dreaming easier to do.

Betty told us about her path to getting in touch with her dream of working with flowers. *"I've led a very interesting life. After university I got a series of progressively better and better jobs. But I married the wrong man. Always listen to your father because he knows. When I was going down the aisle, my father said, 'Say no,' and I said, 'Shh, Dad, I'm the one getting married.' The marriage was not good and the turning point was when my former husband physically threatened me. I called the police. They took him away and they took me to a shelter for battered wives.*

*"When I was at the shelter, I looked around and realized how fortunate I was. I was strong enough and I had a head on my shoulders. I got a restraining order for my husband and three years later I finally got the divorce (but he got the dog, unfortunately). I met a new man who was the complete opposite of my ex-husband. We married and he has taught me much about life and maturity, but I was soul-searching. I had to ensure my own identity and destiny—which I did. I had to get out on my own. So I got my own apartment. We didn't get a divorce. We just separated. I needed to find out who I was. I separated to find myself. My husband was really supportive of*

*me. He said, 'You better do what you have to do, but I will be there.' A number of years later, I said, 'You can come back into my life,' and we've been together ever since. You've got to find out what's inside of you in order to cope."*

Betty continued, "*I really love flowers and plants. It is a passion. Four years ago I took a personal interest in my own garden. I learned a lot. I was self-taught and I started garden-ing. I had an idea for a garden business and I had no fears. So I launched a business of redesigning people's gardens. I started by finding this really neat computer program that shows you how your property will look with each rearrangement of flowers. I never looked back. Last year, I had about ten clients and this year I have about thirty. I feel a major energy surge now and I am burning the candle at both ends. I'm having a blast.*"

Betty is an excellent example of a woman who took back her life and put herself in charge.

There are five prerequisites for dreaming. The very act of putting these prerequisites in place, even one at a time, is a step towards taking charge of your life. The prerequisites for dreaming are

- permission
- time
- place and space
- practice
- coach and fan

**Permission.** Give yourself permission to dream. Dreaming is not a frivolous activity. Many of you put everyone else's needs before your own and believe that taking time for your own needs is an act of self-indulgence or selfishness. You are the same women who eat only the leftovers or make sure that others eat before you sit down to the meal. You are the same women who may have devoted your lives to your husbands or partners, your children, your parents, your jobs. Over the years, you have given short shrift to that part of yourself that would like to dream. That is why giving yourself permission to dream is an important step in the process. Betty gave herself permission to get in touch with who she was when she decided to separate from her second husband.

**Time.** Just as you have to take time to exercise, you have to take time to get in touch with who you are and your dreams. In Chapter 9, we help you to create the road map for achieving your dream. However, you can't reach your dream if you don't know what it is. To get in touch with your dream, you need time for reflection, time to do the exercises in this book and time to think about how you responded. We can't over-emphasize how critical it is that you give yourself time. You see how important "time out" was for Betty.

You may choose to devote a significant amount of time to dreaming like Nicole told us she did. *"After I lost my job, when I wondered what my next step should be, I forbade myself to make a decision. It was summer. I took the summer off. I told myself: 'Do whatever you want but don't think about work. Don't think about the future.' I was very surprised by what I learned during that time: What pleased me, what angered me, what frightened me."*

Set aside time—an hour, a week, a summer off or a full-year sabbatical—for dreaming. If a summer off is not possible, devote small amounts of time each day to think. Going for a walk or meditating are good methods to clear your mind and open yourself to new ideas.

**Place and space.** You need to find a special space for dreaming. This can be indoors or outdoors. The space can be as large as your own room or as small as a special chair that is yours and yours alone. We recommend this because all too often, when you set out to claim territory, there may be a slow, insidious erosion of your space. That favorite chair in a small part of a larger room should have a "Bums Off" sign to protect your thinking space.

Laurie, in anticipation of setting a new direction in her life, built a small room onto her house for herself. She added doors that could close it off from the rest of the house. It is a lovely room with a large picture window that looks out onto the garden. The inspiration for a room of her own overlooking the garden came from a sabbatical she spent in Seattle, a city known for lovely vistas. This sabbatical year also taught her the value of taking time and creating space for thinking and getting in touch with dreams. She wasn't able to build the room immediately. It took her eight years to create the room and "bring Seattle to Montreal."

You may not be able to build a room but you can find a space, even if it is at the library, on a park bench or at the local coffee shop.

**Practice.** For many women, the act of dreaming itself can be foreign and uncomfortable. Don't get discouraged if initially you have difficulty getting in touch with your dreams. The exercise of dreaming, like other forms of exercise, improves with practice. Betty practiced on her own garden and then on her neighbors' gardens, perfecting designs and techniques before turning her dream into reality.

> **Tip:** The first step in practicing dreaming is to jot down notes as they pop into your head. Buy yourself a small notebook or a personal organizer that fits into your pocket. Don't leave a room or home without it.

**Coach and fan.** Everyone needs a coach or a fan in his or her life. You need someone else to listen to you when you cannot hear yourself. At times you may feel overwhelmed by the complexity and magnitude of the task of getting in touch with your dreams. As you delve deeper, things that once looked simple or clear often become complex and foggy. This is the time to call on a friend or family member or a professional whose skill or job is to actively listen. They have to be able to decipher code, note discrepancies in what you are saying and how you behave, and know you well enough to understand what your ideals, values and interests are, and where you want to go.

Deanna played this role with Laurie. Deanna had begun to define her own dream ten months before Laurie had begun to embark on hers. When Laurie was ready to begin thinking about her dream, Deanna served as her coach, helping Laurie outline and articulate what she heard Laurie say was important to her. Because Deanna knew Laurie so well, she knew what questions to ask to help Laurie clarify her thoughts.

> **Tip:** You can also be your own best coach. To do this, you must write things down and then take the time to reread what you have written so that you hear yourself anew. Keep your notebook or a personal organizer close to your pillow. Often, the best ideas pop into your head while you are asleep.

All that said, don't wait for ideal conditions to set out your dream. Indeed, if you wait for ideal conditions you may never get around to dreaming. Another day wasted, another week gone, another postponement in taking charge of your life and living your dreams.

## What Are the Obstacles to Dreaming?

Fears are the major obstacles to dreams. Fears paralyze and undermine self-confidence. All of us have fears, real or imagined. The secret here is to identify your fears and learn how to manage them so that they do not overwhelm you and prevent you from getting on with your dream.

To begin identifying your fears, take your notebook and make a list of what scares you about dreaming.

Here are some of the fears that women shared with us along with some suggested antidotes.

*Fear:* **I don't have a dream or I won't be able to get in touch with my dream.**

*Antidote:* Everyone has a dream. At the very least, everyone has preferences, enjoyments and interests. Simply think of yours. Such preferences are some of the ingredients of dreams. The first step is to get in touch with these ingredients, which we help you to do with the exercises in Chapter 3.

**Fear: I am so afraid I will fail. I feel paralyzed.**

*Antidote:* Separate dreaming into two steps. The first is to create the dream regardless of whether you think you can do it or not. The second is to figure out how you can do it. Start with step one and don't worry or even think about step two until you are in touch with the dream. Taking the first step brings you closer to where you want to be.

Also, try to manage the fear by asking yourself: "What is the worst thing that can happen? Can I live with that? If I don't do it, will I look back with regret?"

**Fear: I'm afraid that if I commit to my dream I won't be able to or won't want to see it through.**

*Antidote:* You may decide to keep your dream a secret until you've tested the waters and you feel comfortable with your decision. The water will seem less frigid once you have waded in, and you may soon find yourself proudly talking about the dream.

**Fear: I am afraid I will be disappointed by my dream.**

*Antidote:* So what? You don't have to be perfect. It's better to do something than to do nothing. And once you have started to do something, any activity is a work in progress which can be continually improved and altered.

*Fear:* **I am afraid I will choose the wrong path.**

*Antidote:* There are no wrong paths, just new directions. Even if you are on a path that doesn't fit, you can always change direction. You have learned something along that path that will help you make better decisions in the future.

*Fear:* **My dream is a fantasy and I will never make it happen.**

*Antidote:* Remember dreams are not fantasies. The best way to turn a fantasy into an achievable dream is to write it down. Look at it. Figure out why you think it's impossible and try to eliminate those aspects. The fantasy will soon metamorphose into a real dream.

For many women, the fear of regret overrides other fears and serves to motivate them to action. Fear of not having taken advantage of an opportunity can be very powerful. This fear, in fact, is more acutely felt during the Vantage Years because you are more aware of the passing of time.

Most of the women we interviewed spoke of how they overcame the fear of taking action by recognizing that what they feared more was *not* taking action.

Sara told us about her fear of regret and how she learned to manage it. *"I had more fears about transitions when I was much younger. I was much more fearful of leaping into the unknown in my twenties and even in the beginning of my thirties than I have been in the past few years. I had this moment of realization that resonated with me. I had been divorced and I had no children. When I got tenure at the university, I felt I was in a position to raise a child alone. I could be financially as well as emotionally responsible. I thought about having a child and I had repeated conversations in my head, the yes, the no, and then it struck me. I had no regrets in my life about anything I had ever done. Not that I had never made mistakes that I had to account for and deal with and correct, but all my regrets were about things that I had hesitated over. I thought to myself—'At the end of my days I don't want to regret not having had the courage of my convictions.' I knew I wouldn't regret creating a situation that might be hard for me or where I had to work hard or have less money than I wanted or a whole host of things that are part of life's struggle. I wouldn't regret having those difficulties, but I would regret having missed something that I really wanted and not having done what was in my power.*

"When I embraced that thought of becoming a single mother, it not only helped me with the decision that I had at hand but I think it carried over to other things. What stayed with me was that sense of not being afraid to make the best decision I can make: right or wrong, or partly right or partly wrong. Everything changes once you act and then you see what you have to do next."

You are now ready to take the first step—getting in touch with your dreams.

three

# GETTING IN TOUCH WITH YOUR DREAMS

*Dreams are faithful interpretations of our inclinations:*
*But there is art required to sort and understand them.*
                    —MONTAIGNE, "Of Experience."[1]

YOU KNOW NOW HOW CRITICAL dreams are in your life.
Now that you have given yourself permission, set aside time
and found a place and space, you are ready to practice
dreaming. You also now recognize your fears and are working on managing them. It is a bonus if you have found yourself a coach and fan.

    In this chapter we have designed several exercises to get
you in touch with your dreams.

    Keep the following in mind to help you get started and
stay on course.

Remember that a dream must

- be something that matters to you.
- be concordant with your values.
- capture your passions.
- reflect your interests.
- make you feel good about yourself.

A dream does NOT

- have to be a calling.
- have to be big to be called a dream.
- need to be too specific.
- need to be complete or perfect—it's a work in progress.

Remember that a dream is *not* the plan. You are six chapters away from creating your personal road map.

You know that it is the right dream and you are on the right track when the dream

- feels right.
- makes you proud to talk about it.
- fills you with a sense of excitement.
- renews your hope for the future.
- brings fulfillment.

One of the simplest ways to get in touch with your dreams is to revisit the dreams of your youth: "I always wanted to be an actress." "I always wanted to have a meaningful family life." "I always wanted to feed the poor in Africa."

Ideas of youth are important because youth is the time when you were formulating your identity, unencumbered by adult responsibilities and the other realities of life. Do these dreams still resonate with you? If they do, you may be better equipped now with greater inner strengths (Chapter 5) and more essential resources (Chapter 6) to act on them.

Carley always dreamt of becoming a ballet dancer and she trained from a young age. When it became apparent she was never going to be a ballet star, she was adamant about not giving up her dream. In rethinking her dream, she had to ask herself a basic question—*"What is it about ballet that I truly love or that truly appeals to me?"* In answering the question, to her surprise, she realized that she was passionate about movement and that ballet was simply an expression of this passion. She began to explore other ways of expressing her passion of movement. She discovered yoga and Pilates, and is now enrolled in a master's program in kinesiology. She still dances every day, finding a new way to express her dream.

Another way to get in touch with your dreams is to think of three categories of dreams:

- Dreams about me
- Dreams about relationships and community
- Dreams about the world

We have taken inspiration for our categories from two notable psychologists, Peter Schmuck and Kennon Sheldon, who classified life goals (which we are calling dreams) into three groups: Self-Enhancement Goals; Group Enhancement Goals; and Global Enhancement Goals.[2]

**Dreams about me.** Dreams about me are dreams that relate to your inner life, your creative urges. They involve what you would like to do, who you would like to be, how you would like to behave in your personal and professional life. They are dreams that relate to the development of self and of lifestyle choices. Examples of dreams about me could be:

> I want to pursue my talent in art.
> I want to learn more about philosophy.
> I want to explore the world.
> I want to explore new ideas.

**Dreams about relationships.** Dreams about relationships are dreams that refer to the types of relationships you have or would like to have. Relationships include all members of your social network—from people who are very close and intimate to those who are more distant (family, friends, colleagues, community). Examples of dreams involving relationships could be:

> I want to have a best friend.
> I want to find a new partner.
> I want to contribute to community life.

**Dreams about the world.** Dreams about the world are dreams that relate to doing something for your country, other countries and the world. These dreams refer to how you fit into the broader world. Examples of dreams about the world could be:

> I imagine myself caring for the poor.
> I want to help make the world a safer place.
> I want to help children with special needs.

## Exercises for Getting in Touch with Your Dreams

In this chapter we have designed a series of exercises to get you in touch with your dreams. We have organized the exercises to follow a physical workout: You begin with two warm-up exercises, followed by three main exercises and you conclude with a cool-down. If you already know your dream, you can choose to skip some of these exercises. However, we recommend that you review them to at least validate your dream, because they identify the essential ingredients and the nature of your dream. At the end of this workout, you should know your dream or know the ingredients that are essential to your dream.

Warm-up exercises:
- My Values
- Down Memory Lane

Main exercises:
- Ingredients for a Dream
- Dreams About Me, About Relationships, About the World
- Reflective Dreamer

Cool-down exercise:
- The Authentic Dream

---

## Warm-Up Exercise: My Values

(Time to complete: 10–30 minutes)

Because a good dream must be concordant with your values, the first step in dreaming is to get in touch with your values.

Values are principles and standards that guide your behavior and direct your actions.

*Step 1:* Identify the five or ten values that you feel most define you. Write them down in your notebook.

*Step 2:* Read the My Values checklist on the next page and rate how important each value is to you (high importance, medium importance, low importance).

*Step 3:* Add the ones of high importance to your list of values that define you.

Keep your list of values beside you as you go through the rest of the exercise program to remind yourself what is really important to you, what drives you.

| Values | High | Medium | Low |
|---|---|---|---|
| **MY VALUES** | | | |
| Adventure | | | |
| Aesthetic / Beauty | | | |
| Athleticism | | | |
| Balance | | | |
| Challenge | | | |
| Creativity | | | |
| Environmental sustainability | | | |
| Equality | | | |
| Freedom | | | |
| Fulfillment | | | |
| Fun | | | |
| Growth | | | |
| Health | | | |
| Helping others | | | |
| Honesty / Integrity | | | |
| Independence | | | |
| Intellectual stimulation | | | |
| Love | | | |
| Learning | | | |
| Making a difference | | | |
| Meaningful relationships | | | |
| Money | | | |
| Peace of mind | | | |
| Power | | | |
| Recognition | | | |
| Security and safety | | | |
| Self-expression | | | |
| Self-respect | | | |
| Socialization | | | |
| Spirituality | | | |
| Supportive relationships | | | |

## Warm-up Exercise: Down Memory Lane

(Time to complete: 30 minutes or more)

This warm-up exercise will jog your memory about events in your life that made you happy, brought you pleasure—events that still bring a smile to your face, a small chuckle. You are brainstorming a long list of events. We find that a good way to do this is to do a life review, from early childhood through high-school years, into university and early work experience, marriage, family and job and then into the Vantage Years. For each of these periods, select those events that bring a smile to your face and a warm feeling to your heart. It could be as few as ten or as many as you remember. Consult our example on the next page to get a sense of how to set up your own table and for some ideas to get you started.

> **Tip:** The more events you list, the more ideas you will generate to build a dream. It may help to go through photo albums to remember the highlights of your life.

## EXAMPLE: DOWN MEMORY LANE

| Life Period | Event |
| --- | --- |
| 3 to 10 years | birthday, school play, school outing, sports competition, family vacation, reading a book |
| 10 to 20 years | school event, prom, summer camp, learning to drive, graduation, leaving home, concerts |
| 21 to 26 years | travel, landing a job, first paycheck, romance, moving away, marriage, children, family holidays |
| 27 to 35 years | children, graduation, promotion, travel, buying a house, making a sale, succeeding at a job |
| 36 to 45 years | winning a big deal, completing a project, raising children, involvement in community, volunteering, taking a holiday |
| 45 to 65 years | mentoring, paying off the mortgage, grandchildren |
| 65 + | grandchildren, travel, running a marathon, retiring |

## Main Exercise: The Ingredients for a Dream

(Time to complete: 90–120 minutes)

*Step 1:* From the long list of events generated in Down Memory Lane, select at least five events that gave you a sense of fulfillment, satisfaction—the ones associated with the happiest memories.

*Step 2:* Take each event and write a paragraph or one page about the event. Describe the situation in as much detail as you can recall: the occasion, the people, the place, how you were involved, what made it special for you, how you felt before, during and after the event. Write down why this event was memorable. You are doing this exercise to get in touch with those ingredients that are essential in your life, ingredients that meet your emotional, intellectual, achievement and social needs.

> **Tip:** Remember to be as descriptive as possible. The richness in your description of the event will really show you what ingredients brought you happiness.

**Laurie's example. The event: Having the family come home for Thanksgiving.**

My heart always sings when I get ready for the holidays, and this Thanksgiving was no exception. What I love the most about Thanksgiving is everybody coming home and preparing for the holiday. I love planning the menus keeping each person's favorite foods in mind, creating menus that blend different tastes, textures and colors, experimenting and trying out new recipes, arranging the food in creative and eye-pleasing and aesthetic ways. I enjoy decorating the house, cleaning the silver, setting a beautiful table with my best dishes and linen, buying flowers. I especially enjoy shopping for the food. I love cooking with my daughter, as we research and make up new recipes and discuss how different flavors blend. I love the tasting and the smells. I get excited when everyone arrives and everything is ready and the house looks so festive. I am proud of my home, my culinary talents and my organizational skills. The best part is spending time with the family, seeing them all together and spending special time with my children. I enjoy taking part in the conversations and debates around the table. I get great pleasure from making so many people happy. I get satisfaction when people applaud my talents as a great hostess and cook. I smile to myself because once again, I pulled it off. It all looked so effortless and only I know how much effort it really took.

**Deanna's example. The event: Financing a major acquisition for a company in the oil and gas industry.**

The objective was to structure the financing for the buyer so that the least amount of cash would be necessary to close the deal. I got the most pleasure from leading the deal team and closing the deal. I enjoyed working long hours with the team, creating innovative solutions, negotiating and solving problems. What an adrenaline rush I had in leading the group to victory from winning the mandate, selling the ideas and making them happen. I loved the mental stimulation of creating the solution, the presentation, planning, organizing and implementing. I got great pleasure from teaching, coaching, learning and mentoring. The best part of this experience was when I met with the clients and my team. I got great satisfaction when we congratulated each other on a job well done. I was applauded by others, recognized and financially rewarded for this successful deal. I felt proud that my opinions were valued and the task was worthwhile.

> **Tip:** If you are still having some difficulty composing your paragraph, you may use the sentences below to describe your event.

You want to include in each description of the event sentences like

I got pleasure from . . . because . . .
I felt important when . . . because . . .
I felt loved when . . . because . . .
I felt secure when . . . because . . .
I felt exhilarated when . . . because . . .
I felt rewarded . . . because . . .
I felt satisfied when . . . because . . .
I felt free when . . . because . . .
I get excited about . . . because . . .
I feel proud to talk about . . . because . . .
I feel good about myself when . . . because . . .
I enjoy doing . . . because . . .
I enjoy being recognized for . . . because. . .

*Step 3:* Once your paragraphs on each event are written, you should read each one. Circle or highlight the key words identifying the ingredients that made the event pleasurable for you.

**Laurie's example. The event: Having the family come home for Thanksgiving.**

My heart always sings when I get ready for the holidays, and this Thanksgiving was no exception. What I love the most about Thanksgiving is **everybody coming home** and **preparing for the holiday**. I love **planning the menus** keeping each person's favourite foods in mind, **creating** menus that blend different tastes, textures and colors, **experimenting** and **trying out** new recipes, arranging the food in creative and **eye-pleasing and aesthetic ways**. I enjoy **decorating** the house, cleaning the silver, setting a beautiful table with my best dishes and linen, buying **flowers**. I especially enjoy **shopping** for the food. I love **cooking with my daughter**, as we research and make up new recipes and **discuss** how different flavours blend. I love the tasting and the smells. I get excited when everyone arrives and everything is ready and the house looks so festive. I am **proud** of my home, my **culinary talents** and my **organizational skills**. The best part is **spending time with the family**, seeing them all together, and spending special time with my children. I enjoy taking part in the **conversations and debates** around the table. I get great pleasure from **making so many people happy**. I get satisfaction when **people applaud my talents** as a great hostess and cook. I smile to myself because once again, I pulled it off. It all **looked so effortless** and only I know how much effort it really took.

**Deanna's example. The event: Financing a major acquisition for a company in the oil and gas industry.**

The objective was to structure the financing for the buyer so that the least amount of cash would be necessary to **close the deal**. I got the most pleasure from **leading the deal team** and closing the deal. I enjoyed **working** long hours **with the team**, **creating innovative solutions, negotiating and solving problems**. What an **adrenaline rush** I had in leading the group to victory from winning the mandate, **selling** the ideas and making them happen. I loved the mental stimulation of creating the solution, the presentation, planning, **organizing** and **implementing**. I got great pleasure from **teaching**, **coaching**, **learning and mentoring**. The best part of this experience was when I met with the **clients** and my team. I got great satisfaction when we **congratulated** each other on a job well done. I was **applauded by others**, **recognized and financially rewarded** for this successful deal. I felt proud that my **opinions were valued** and the **task was worthwhile**.

*Step 4:* Repeat steps 1, 2 and 3 for each event that you have described. Now you have circled or highlighted many words. These words are the ingredients needed to build your dream.

*Step 5:* To find out which are the most significant ingredients, or the elements that give you the most satisfaction, create a grid. Place your ingredients at the top of the columns and your five to ten events in rows along the side (see the example on the next page). You should have ten to fifteen columns and five to ten rows. Now place Xs in the boxes where the ingredient was part of the event.

*Step 6:* Add up the Xs to determine which ingredients occurred in most, or all, of your pleasurable events. Those are the ingredients that have worked for you in the past.

| | In charge | Creative | Social contact | Recognition | Time for myself, etc. |
|---|---|---|---|---|---|
| **EXAMPLE: INGREDIENTS** | | | | | |
| Fifth birthday party | | | X | X | |
| Trip to Argentina | | | X | | |
| Giving a speech | | X | X | X | |
| Walking alone in the early morning | X | | | | X |
| Birth of a child | | | X | X | |
| Making a sale | | X | | | |
| TOTAL | I | 2 | 4 | 3 | I |
| Level of import-ance today | *** | *** | ** | ** | * |

*Step 7:* Using the rating scale below, decide which ingredients your dream must have, which ones would be nice to have but are not essential, and which ones you could leave out at this time. Ask yourself, How important is each of

these ingredients for me today, and add the appropriate number of stars.

Rating scale:

3 stars (***):  The ingredient is very important and it is a "must-have" for my dream.

2 stars (**):   The ingredient is still important and although I would like it to be part of my dream, it is a "nice-to-have" but not essential.

1 star (*):     The ingredient may be important but it can be saved for another dream.

If you look at the example, the ingredient "in charge," though it only appeared in one event, was very important— a "must-have." It is possible that ingredients that were important to you in the past are no longer so.

---

You should now have a heightened awareness of the ingredients that are needed in your dreams. Any dream you choose must include the "must-have" ingredients and some of the "nice-to-have" ingredients. These are the ingredients that will help you choose a dream that will resonate with who you are and give your life meaning, purpose and joy.

We illustrate what you have just done with the following, very simple, baking example. If you have seven "must-have" ingredients: fat, eggs, sweetener, flour, flavoring, liquid and a leavening agent, you can bake an endless array of goodies— cakes, cookies, breads, muffins, scones and so on.

Now let's get back to your dream. You have assembled all your ingredients and now you have to decide what form your dream will take. No doubt some ideas for dreams have come into your head. You might create a short list of dreams and keep them close to you in your notebook. To help you create this list, complete the following two exercises.

---

## Main Exercise: Dreams About Me, Dreams About Relationships, Dreams About the World

(Time to complete: 60 minutes)

Remember back to the Categories of Dreams from the start of the chapter: Dreams about Me, Dreams about Relationships, Dreams About the World. Now complete the following sentences in your own notebook.

Dreams about me
    I want to pursue . . .
    I want to learn more about . . .
    I want to become . . .
    I want to achieve . . .
    I want to be in control of . . .

Dreams about relationships
    I want to contribute . . .
    I want to be respected by . . .
    I want to be a better . . .
    I want to find . . .

Dreams about the world
    I envision a world . . .

I would like to help . . .
I want to contribute . . .

---

## Main Exercise: Reflective Dreamer
(Time to complete: 120 minutes)

In this exercise, you will use for inspiration the same list of events that you generated for the Down Memory Lane exercise. If you have thought of other events, add them to the list now. If you are satisfied that your list is comprehensive, remind yourself of these happy events by reading them aloud.

Then write a three- to ten-sentence answer for each question below. The answers to these reflective questions will identify potential dreams. You can make your answers as sketchy or as detailed as you want.

- What is important to me?
- If I could do anything, what would I love to do? What is the most appealing part of that activity for me?
- What is a "great" day for me?
- What would I like a headline to say about me?
- What work or play do I find so enjoyable that the hours pass quickly?
- What were the things I did in my youth that I found most enjoyable or that made me feel fulfilled or brought me satisfaction?
- What are the things I have done in my life that have made me most proud?
- What words best describe who I really am?

- What would I do if I had more time?
- What would I do to make my life better? other peoples' lives better?

> **Tip: Write down the first answers you think of rather than second-guessing yourself. Then come back to your answers in a few days and refine them.**

Sue, in searching for her dream, began by asking herself two reflective questions: *"What do I do that makes my life better? How can I help other people to make their lives better?' I notice that my life is better because I am organized. Everybody's lives can be improved by learning at least some method of being more organized. I am a teacher by profession and I began to believe that organization can be taught and people trained. I teach people how to organize themselves, their homes, their lives. Some of the women I have helped through my business live totally overwhelmed by their disorganization—marriages are affected, children are affected. These people can't see the light of day. I go into their homes and their lives, and almost every single day I have a positive success story where somebody calls to thank me."*

---

It is at this time that some of you might fall into the BUT trap. "Oh, that idea is good BUT . . ." This is *not* the time to limit possibilities. Consider even the most far-fetched idea. You will have plenty of time as you go through the book to pare down your list of what you can or cannot do as you get more in touch with you dream and learn more about yourself. Now is the time to entertain all ideas and to stay open-minded.

Remember, too, that dreams can take many forms. If your dream is to help the elderly, you may do it in a variety of ways— working with the elderly to create their own gardens, opening up a taxi service to drive the elderly to appointments, visiting seniors in hospital, doing their hair and nails and so on—as long as each form contains your must-have ingredients. If your dream is to be a gardener, you may want to help the elderly in their gardens. You may want to create your own beautiful garden. You may be involved in beautifying highways, and so on.

Hold that sigh of relief. You still need a cool-down to validate your dreams.

---

## Cool-down Exercise: The Authentic Dream
(Time to complete: 30 minutes or less)

To be authentic, your dream must incorporate many or most of your "must-have" ingredients. Sue's dream of running a business to organize others incorporates her "must-have" ingredients of being in charge, organizing, teaching and helping others.

Look at your "must-have" ingredients and assess whether your dream incorporates all of them.

In order for a dream to be authentic it must also satisfy the requirements outlined in Chapter 2. For each possible dream, assess the degree to which it meets the requirements of a good or authentic dream. Do this by completing the table on the next page.

> **Tip: You may need to make copies of the table because you need a copy for each possible dream.**

| Requirements of a Dream | THE AUTHENTIC DREAM | | |
|---|---|---|---|
| | Strongly Agree | Somewhat Agree | Disagree |
| Meaningful to me | | | |
| Consistent with my values | | | |
| Resonates with who I really am | | | |
| Mine, not somebody else's | | | |
| Gives direction for my future | | | |
| Realistic | | | |
| Captures my passions and interests | | | |
| Makes me feel good about myself | | | |
| Makes me feel joyful and glad | | | |

Check off the statements in the table above. If you strongly agree, give yourself two points; somewhat agree, one point; disagree, zero. Tally up your points.

If your total score is between:

14–18   Congratulations! You have found your authentic dream and you are on your way.

8–13   You are almost at your authentic dream, but check what requirements are not being met. Your score suggests that you have some requirements but not all. Look over each item to see what characteristic your dream is not satisfying. For example, if the score for the item "consistent with my values" is low, you could repeat the My Values exercise on page 59.

0–7    You have not yet tapped into your authentic dream. But do not worry—these things take time.

---

Well done! You should now have your authentic dream or a few potential authentic dreams that include your "must-have" ingredients. At the very least, you have identified, articulated and validated the ingredients that are essential for your dream.

> **Tip: Create a Dream Sheet. Write down your dream, and the elements your dream must include, in a special place that is portable and accessible. Laurie buys mini notebooks that fit into her pocket, whereas Deanna carries around one scrappy piece of paper printed from her personal organizer. As you read through the book you will have an opportunity to add insights.**

You have a vision for your future direction. You are now ready to continue your journey of discovery. But to take charge of your life and live your dream, you first need to understand the process of transition that all women go through during the Vantage Years. We call this process of transition the Vantage Process. It helps to know where you are in the process because only by moving through its phases can you achieve your dream. In the next chapter you will see that creating a dream is a critical phase in the Vantage Process.

four

# THE VANTAGE PROCESS:
# WHERE ARE YOU?

GWEN IS CONTEMPLATING RETIRING. *"My current job is as a stockbroker in a major investment firm. I had spent most of my career at a large accounting firm as a partner. Although I've always enjoyed all the work that I've done and I've had a very interesting career, I have come to the conclusion that work interferes with my life. I'm actually looking forward to the possibility of retiring at fifty-five. A lot of people say to me, 'Well, what are you going to do? You've always been so busy.' That is the least of my worries."*

Elaine C., an educator, had a well-thought-out plan that took a bend in the road. *"I had a plan that I'd work for ten more years and then I'd retire. By then I'd be ready to do some consulting. My plan was to be in the driver's seat. I had been in a new position for six years when I found myself faced with another transition. This was the fourth board chairperson within six years and we didn't get along. The board and I came to an agreement that I would leave after one more year. But I had a choice about how to manage this year: Do I work hard or not? I learned a lot about myself during this year of transition. I had a lot of anger. The first two months I didn't do very much of anything at all. I just had to get to a place of acceptance. I engaged an executive coach. It was a smart and healthy thing to do. I spent time figuring out what I wanted to do next. The hard part was working full-time. I worked very, very long days. Living twenty-five miles away from the school, leaving home early in the morning and often not getting home before 10:30 or 11:00 at night. But it was important to me."* Elaine wanted to leave her position feeling that she had accomplished something of significance. *"I had to find another position before I left. I needed to be able to leave and say, 'I'm going to a new job.' I'm happy to say I got a position as an associate director. Somebody called me and said, 'I think you're the right person for this job.'"*

Betsy, a recently retired corporate executive, explained: *"I have been working in financial services for thirty-six years. I never worked anywhere for more than five years, and usually within the five years at each organization I did two or three different jobs. I got fired once, downsized twice. I probably reinvented myself the most after I was fired. It was a very, very difficult thing. I was in a very senior position. It was really a tough experience. It's not fun. Then I had to go find a new job, which I did, and I had a great time at that job until we got sold. Then I went on to help another company sell itself. I no longer want to work in a place where you 'eat what you kill,' where you are only as good as your next deal. Nor do I want something where you are on 24/7. I really don't want to do it anymore."*

Beverly describes what happened when teachers were offered early-retirement packages. *"I was in Australia at the time when the government offered unbelievable retirement packages. I accepted the package even though I was fifty-five at the time. I was devastated, thinking, 'What am I going to do?' I took French courses, got research assistant jobs that have been fascinating. I needed to feel productive. I needed to be challenged. I now work part-time and travel. I am enjoying less pressure, no guilt. I needed balance and now I have it."*

Janet, at thirty-five, has made the decision to stay home after the birth of her second child in three years. *"I am torn between my desire to care for my children full-time or to return to work. My husband wants me to stay at home, whereas I am not sure that's best for me. I am afraid that I will not be challenged and that I won't feel I am doing my bit. I don't know what to do."*

These women describe major events, some planned, some unplanned, which they will look back on as turning points in their lives. These turning points can occur between careers, between work situations, from work to traditional or nontraditional retirement, or from the role of homemaker to a new adventure. Turning points serve as catalysts or triggers to drive change and promote growth. Turning points are prime times for revisiting dreams and getting in touch with dreams because they give you the opportunity to think about the future. However, too often we become so anxious to get through this period of transition that we don't give ourselves the time to stop and plan for the future, and so the future just happens to us. The Vantage Years can be a time to go through this process more consciously and create the future you want for yourself.

Regardless of who you are or what events you are living through, there are several distinct phases involved in any kind of transition. In this chapter you will learn about these phases and how the transition process works. You will learn that all transitions—such as having a child, changing jobs, divorcing, retiring, moving house—have much in common. At the same time, each transition has its own particular characteristics because of the unique challenges and tasks inherent in that event.

In this chapter you will learn the answers to these questions:

- What is a transition?
- What is the Vantage Process?
- Why is it necessary to view a transition as a process?
- What are the five phases of the Vantage Process?
- How can I successfully transition through the Vantage Process?

## What Is a Transition?

A transition is when you move from one situation to a new situation. A transition is a turning point, a point of reference from which your life takes a new direction and takes on new meaning. This new direction requires that you adapt or change by restructuring relationships, responsibilities and roles. In addition to a change in behavioral responses and new roles, this new direction also requires that you set new goals and rework your identity.[1] This is where dreaming and dreams come into play. The transitional events most often experienced during the Vantage Years are career changes, retirement, illness, deaths, children leaving home and becoming a grandparent.

The process of transition at midlife, which we have called the Vantage Process, involves reappraising, retooling, reinventing, reenergizing, rewiring, refocusing, resetting direction and revving all engines to full speed ahead. It does not mean retreating. Getting in touch with your dreams and knowing how you want to spend these years is an integral part of this process and determines how successfully you will come through this period in your life.

Some people anticipate these changes and prepare themselves as well as they can. Others do not see the early warning signals and may find themselves ill-prepared.

## What Is the Vantage Process?

We call the process of transitioning at this stage of life the Vantage Process because you need to find a new vantage point from which to dream.

You do come to this process with a decided advantage. Over the first half of your life you have developed many strengths that you can use to write new scripts and create new meaning and direction for your life. This is the central work of the Vantage Process. It is hardly surprising that this work can elicit a wide range of emotions from anxiety, depression, anger, guilt to joy, happiness, elation. These emotions vary in intensity, may be transitory or may last longer than any of you would like or expect. For some, the process is a crisis and for others it is less traumatic.

There are five phases in the Vantage Process and everyone goes through all the phases. For some women one phase may last a long time while for another it may fly by. Rest assured, you will make it through. The Vantage Process should not only be viewed as a means to an end; you should also enjoy the journey. It provides you with an important opportunity to explore new ideas and different ways of doing things. For many of you, it will be a transformational experience, altering your life and unleashing new potential. The process can be terrifying but it also can be exhilarating.

Home-oriented women may find themselves at a crossroad when children leave home. Work-oriented women may face job boredom, layoffs and increasing difficulty in finding the next job. Many women over forty are surprised to find they are dealing with these unanticipated transitions before they had expected to, with little or no preparation.

Libby describes how she took advantage of an opportunity without knowing what she was going to do next: *"I was an international banker for twenty-four years. I had a great career in banking and when my bank was taken over by another bank, the severance packages were extremely generous and I really wanted to do something different. I took the package. I got out free and clear. My title intact, my experience intact and all my memories intact."* Yet Libby was unprepared for what was to come next. The job and volunteer opportunities in many fields were limited and certainly not age neutral. Libby continues: *"After about eight months, my counselor in outplacement said, 'You've got to fish or cut bait. You're not getting any bites. It's very hard to break into a completely new field.'"* Libby was counseled to make a new plan as the old avenues were no longer open.

The real work of the Vantage Process is not simply in transitioning from one situation to the next, but also in evolving as an individual. It is not simply about finding a new job. It is about deciding who you are and what type of life you want to live—directed by your dreams.

## Why Is It Necessary to View This Transition as a Process?

Being fired or retired or feeling mired in your job or at home is the beginning of the process, not the end of your life. Viewing what you are going through as a process rather than as series of discrete, isolated, unconnected incidents may prevent you from becoming overwhelmed. Unless you understand that this is a process, it is difficult to take charge, but take charge you must! When you understand that you are going through a process, you can respect the process and move forward—from confusion to confidence.

Today is the first day of the rest of your life if you

- Recognize that you are particularly receptive and open to new ideas at this time.
- View this period as an opportunity for growth—to learn new roles and new skills, develop new relationships, assume new responsibilities, and find new meaning and new dreams in your life.
- Recognize that there are different ways to go through the process. There is no one right way. You have to find the way that best suits your style. We will give you hints that we and other women have found helpful. However, you are the only one who can tailor these hints to your particular pattern of dealing with the work in each phase of the Vantage Process.
- Recognize that there are issues that need attention and feelings to resolve in each phase. Take time to deal with these issues. Do not ignore them. Unresolved

issues never disappear; they will just resurface, usually at the next turning point in your life.

- Outline your dreams and identify your inner strengths and ensure that you've built up resources that will help you to fulfill your dreams.
- Become aware that you may get stuck and when you do, you may have to make adjustments and repairs. Each obstacle or hurdle might need a different approach. If your wheels are superficially stuck in the snow or mud, your car might need just a little rocking or a push from friends or passersby. On the other hand, if the wheels are deeply embedded in the snow or mud, it may be that only a tow truck can release your car. Similarly, if you are stuck, you might need the help of family and friends. On the other hand, if you are spinning your wheels, you might call on a professional to help you deal with some of your unresolved issues.

## What Are the Five Phases of the Vantage Process?

Phase 1: Recognizing the early warning signals
Phase 2: Saying goodbye
Phase 3: Existing betwixt and between
Phase 4: Creating the dream
Phase 5: Living the dream.

Before we describe each phase, here's a note of explanation on how the process operates. First, as you move through the phases of the process, you gather strength. The past is incorporated into the present and both are woven to become the future. But life does not proceed in a linear, orderly or predictable way. Although the overarching idea is to move forward, you should feel you can move backwards without losing ground. In fact, you can even have each foot in a different phase.

Second, there is no time limit on any phase. A phase might last a few days for some, and for others, months or even years. Even within a phase, the time is variable. It may take at least six months to prepare to leave a situation and many more months to decide what to do next.

Like other transition processes (getting married, having children, losing a loved one, starting a new job), the Vantage Process from beginning to end may take from three to seven years. For those of you who are tempted to close the book now because you don't want to wait that long, please don't give up. Get started. You may even look back and see that you actually began this process a few years ago and are already well on your way. This process does not and should not consume every waking moment of your life. It's just there. You do have other priorities in your life aside from making this transition.

Finally, you should consider that the process is not simply about transitioning "from" something. It is as important to understand the transition "to" something. When Deanna left her full-time job at the bank, she planned to tackle her "When I Have Time" list, and she did. That is why we have asked you to get in touch with your dream at the beginning of the book and keep your dream front and center.

Each phase in the Vantage Process involves an identity statement, a major task to accomplish, emotional responses and behavioral strategies.

## Phase 1: Recognizing the Early Warning Signals

**Identity statement:** *I am my job (teacher, banker, administrative assistant, president, doctor, lawyer, mother, wife, caregiver).*

**Task:** *To watch for early signals of change, both from within and without.*

**Emotional Response:** *Shock, anger, anxiety.*

**Strategy:** *To withdraw or ignore or prepare.*

Life does not feel quite right. Your first inkling that all is not well may come from your own intuition or from an outside event or from a flash of inspiration. Most of us stay in a work situation or in a home situation as long as the conditions satisfy some basic needs: personal safety and financial security, meaning and significance, stimulation and challenge. When some or many of these needs are being met, the tendency is to not rock the boat. In fact, many people expend a great deal of energy keeping the boat steady. This may be the result of inertia or simply fear of the unknown.

But whether you like it or not, the weather does change and you have to respond. Just as you look to a weather report to decide if you should carry an umbrella, you need to take a reading of your work or home situation. In the same way as a storm can slowly gather momentum, you may feel the inklings that it is time for a change, time to move on. You may be feeling that you are a "has been" or that you are letting life just pass you by.

For many of you in the corporate world, the most obvious signals are downsizing, closures and mergers.

Some of the other early warning signals at work may be:

- My ideas are discounted, devalued or ignored.
- I am given work that isn't challenging.
- I have trouble making decisions and I find I second-guess myself.
- I am not having fun anymore.
- I feel jealous of other people's jobs or of colleagues who are more successful.
- My boss is hinting that my pension is sufficient to enjoy playing golf or bridge.
- My company merges or is bought out.
- They move my office to the storeroom and take away my wastepaper basket.
- I notice I live for the weekend, when I can do the things I really enjoy.
- I find myself dreaming about a different future.

Some of the early signals at home may be:

- I feel I have too much free time.
- My children are more self-sufficient.
- I feel my spirit is dying.
- I'm having trouble sleeping or I am sleeping too much.
- My partner plans to retire shortly.
- My partner is preoccupied at work.
- My parent or relative is ailing or has died.
- My friends are traveling.
- I feel anxious and am not happy with my life.
- I keep thinking, I've always wanted to . . .

These signals cause you to experience a degree of discomfort, anger, frustration, shock, anxiety and depression, and undermine your confidence and sense of self. You begin to question your abilities, your significance and your importance. You begin to feel marginalized. Where once you felt that you were in the right place, you now almost have no place, no sense of belonging. You are not feeling comfortable. What once excited you no longer excites. It is time to move on.

Your identity is defined by what you do: I am an accountant, I am a social worker, I am a librarian, I am a daughter, I am a mother, I am a wife, I am a friend. You have defined yourself in terms of your occupation and your job—in terms of the roles you filled. As any aspect of your identity is slowly eroded, you find yourself trying to hold on. You hold on to the status quo by trying to plug the holes in the dike. You try to fix things piecemeal, failing to see how they are part of an emerging pattern of discontent.

You preserve the status quo until something happens and the storm erupts. An event—major or minor—a remark by somebody, something you've read, something you've seen—or just about anything can trigger the realization that the status quo is no longer working for you. Women we spoke to referred to these "happenings" as catalytic because they forced them to face the fact that something was seriously wrong.

These catalysts come in many different forms. It could be as obvious as being fired, severed or abandoned in some way. The death of a loved one is the ultimate catalytic event. But a minor incident can be equally compelling. Although she had been unhappy, Ruth did not quit her job as a community mental health psychologist until they took away her privileged parking spot. On the surface, her response might look like an overreaction to this relatively minor event. But coming on the heels of a series of warning signals, losing her parking spot told Ruth that it was time to move on.

Odette, an entrepreneur in retail, described her early warning signals: *"I was not happy anymore with what I did at work. I didn't feel good about it. I had no more passion. I was not excited. At forty I decided I didn't want to be the buyer and designer any longer. I was traveling the world. People were telling me that I had the best job and I was so lucky. It was supposed to be heaven but it was not. I had a lump in my throat a lot of the time. These were the signals for me. I felt them in my body, in my emotions. It was eating me up. And then I knew I had to make a change. Life is very intelligent. It keeps sending you all these signals to wake you up, until you wake up and understand it's time for a change."*

Once you begin to have such feelings, ignoring them is no longer an effective strategy. It is time to get in tune with what these signals mean by taking heed and changing course.

But first you have to say goodbye to the old ways.


## Phase 2: Saying Goodbye

**Identity Statement:** *I am a loser; I feel like a failure.*
**Task:** *To mourn the losses.*
**Emotional Response:** *Isolation, panic, shock, anxiety, depression.*
**Strategy:** *To withdraw or reflect.*

Once you have become aware that it is time to change, whether by a slow accrual of signs or by a full-blown crisis, you begin to realize that there is no other way out but out. So begins the phase of coming to terms with what has happened to you. It is not only saying goodbye to the situation, but also saying goodbye to other expectations you had for yourself and, in some ways, to your old self. Even though you have recognized the signals, such recognition only prepares you; it doesn't make it easier.

Saying goodbye may involve leaving a situation either physically or figuratively. It may not be as definite as quitting your job or walking out on your family. But it always involves saying goodbye to parts of the old you or goodbye to your old ways of doing things: who you were, the roles you occupied in your home or in the workplace or the way you acted within these roles, the responsibilities that you had, the status that you enjoyed, the relationships that you made, your ways of relating.

If leaving was unplanned, unanticipated or unexpected, as in the case of an early, forced retirement from work or a divorce, your response may be more emotional and intense than if the leaving was planned, anticipated, expected, desired and initiated by you. In any case, you still have to go through a period of adjusting to the loss, of saying goodbye to other people and to specific aspects of yourself.

Premature retirement from work, for whatever reason, is traumatic. It can be especially traumatic for career- and work-oriented women who sacrificed family life for their jobs and who may feel particularly vulnerable. It can be equally traumatic for women who have worked hard at "having it all," combining career and family life. Their work occupied a major part of their life, making the loss all the more significant.

Nicole told us: *"At fifty, I started hearing them . . . the jokes in the office. The little comments about women at fifty and menopause. It was very, very nasty. When I started going to headhunters and for job interviews . . . it was 'My God,' a big sigh, 'What are we going to do with you?' I didn't fit any patterns. I had studied translation, I also got a diploma in executive management. I had become a vice president at the agency. Basically, I was made to feel that my life was over. 'You're not an interesting candidate. Women your age who have lost their jobs, we don't have anything for you.' So I went home and sat in my garden for two months. I learned that you will recover. There is life after fifty but I didn't see it for quite a long time. It was the most shocking period of my life. It all happened at once: I turned fifty, my son left home, it was the end of a love relationship, my job left me, my youth left me because I went into menopause—all in the same twelve-month period. I didn't think I was going to survive. I remember saying to some friends of mine, 'I am nobody. I don't have a job.' I defined myself by my job. It had become very important in my life. The idea that you can't have a different life after you've had a prestigious job and all that comes with that job is just not so."*

Some women have described the loss of a job or position as akin to losing a limb. Many confess that they felt like a failure, a loser. These women attributed these feelings to the loss of identity rather than just the loss of position.

You are surprisingly vulnerable during this period. Many old insecurities tend to resurface. You may go back to some previous identities that haunted you in adolescence: You really are the lazy person that the high-school teacher told your mother that you were. You really are a fraud and everyone has found out.

This sense of loss can also be because you have not fulfilled a dream or achieved a goal by this age. Adolescence and your early-adult years are a time when you create dreams around ambition. You may have had aspirations that you now believe you will never achieve. You dreamt of writing an important book or designing a signature building or having children—and have yet to do this. Some of you have already reconciled yourself to unrealized ambition. Heather summarized these feelings: *"I may have wanted to be queen of the world but perhaps it's OK to be deputy and that's fine. It's not passively accepting this fact. For me, acceptance is a really dynamic, mature, more realistic way of coming to terms with reality and who I am."*

On the other hand, some of you may have more difficulty living with aspirations as yet unattained. Odette described an unrealized dream: *"To me it's like death, when you have a dream that you didn't realize . . . you have to grieve the loss of the dream. It is only when you grieve the loss that you can move on."*

Loss, in our society, is usually associated with the death of a beloved person. Such a loss is acknowledged and legitimized by society and has mourning rituals attached to it. In the case of the loss of a job or early retirement, there are few rituals to follow. In fact, few people see other forms of leave-taking in terms of loss and mourning. When you are downsized, most companies don't even give you the gold watch or retirement party. Children leave home with hardly a wave goodbye. But in fact, these events are losses and an appropriate mourning period may be necessary.

For some of you, your job title was "you" and you may fear that without a job, people will stop recognizing you. You have lost a major part of your identity. It is not surprising that this loss can trigger feelings of shock, anger, depression, anxiety or even an internal crisis. Don't minimize the feelings associated with this phase. If the change is of your own choosing you may be surprised by the fact that these feelings are still present.

In order to get on with your life, it is critical to recognize, acknowledge and mourn what you have lost. Don't be in a hurry to move on before you have given yourself a chance to say goodbye.

While you are still working in the company or institution, you may find that you want to isolate yourself because you feel you no longer belong. You may avoid going to the cafeteria. You may enter the building through the back door, coming in early and leaving late, or coming in late and leaving early. Once you have left your job, for whatever reason, you may find yourself contacting former colleagues, trying to find out what is happening at work. Once your children are gone you may find yourself at loose ends, checking for their e-mails and voice messages.

This phase is important in the Vantage Process because mourning allows you to put distance between what was and what will be. Feeling depressed forces you to take time out. The behavioral strategies of withdrawing, reflecting and mourning give you needed distance. The farther you get from the event, the more the memory fades, the more the pain dulls. The event, the people and the past begin to recede.

Even if you were prepared, you still have to separate from the old and say goodbye before you can move on to the next phase. Generally, this is a short phase but a phase that cannot, and should not, be avoided. Nicole took to her bed and then retreated to her garden for the summer before she could think about moving on. If you short-change this phase of the process you might find yourself needing to spiral back at a later time to deal with unresolved issues. Kristy told us, *"I took the year off after I was downsized, and it took that long for the reality to sink in."*

You know that you are ready to move into the next phase when you once again recognize that you have worth. You know that you are ready when deep down you believe that no one can take away the skills, knowledge, reputation and professional acumen that you have acquired. Not the loss of title, the loss of job or the loss of role can take these valuable qualities away from you.

For those of you who are experiencing prolonged mourning, you have to fight the urge to withdraw, beat up on yourself or blame the world. Often you feel stuck, paralyzed and anxious. You can't move forward because you don't know how to proceed and you feel lost. These are signals that you need help, perhaps from a professional.

While mourning the losses is critical, it should not become all-consuming. At some point you need to stop feeling miserable and begin to move on. The best way to do that is to start thinking about what you want to do next. The best way to think about what to do next is to get in touch with your dreams.

There are many useful strategies to help you say goodbye. And the best one is the Boy Scouts' motto—Be prepared.

Being prepared for as many eventualities as possible is one of the best ways to successfully deal with transition. That is why there are so many preparation classes—premarital classes, prenatal classes, parenting classes.

You may have time to prepare to leave or you may not. If you do have time to prepare, it might help you in coming to terms with the loss. You may want to leave a legacy, leave on good terms or simply leave a tidy shop.

The women we interviewed found that anticipating change in their work or personal life and preparing for it helped them to say goodbye. Here are some of the strategies that worked for them.

- **Establish a leaving date.** By selecting a specific date, you send the message to yourself and to others that you will be leaving. This date gives you and others time to slowly adjust to the change.
- **Plan for a successor.** If you are leaving a job at your discretion, you may be concerned about deserting the ship. Many women find their own successors. When Laurie decided not to take on a second term as director of the School of Nursing at McGill University, she was instrumental in recruiting her successor.
- **Leave a legacy.** Many women want to leave their mark. As Heidi told us, *"Knowing I was planning to leave gave me a sense of urgency to get a project I had always wanted to do off the ground."* Without her intervention, the project would have been a "no-go."
- **Prepare your environment.** Many people renovate their homes or buy that dreamed-of retirement home a few years before actually leaving their position. They create a refuge, a comfortable retreat. Elaine C. bought a cottage in the Berkshires when preparing for the next stage of her life.

- **Create a safety net.** When you are preparing to move from one job into the uncertainty of no job—"no man's land"—you may be taking a leap of faith. What stops many women from taking this leap is very often financial insecurity. In deciding whether or not to leave her university position, Kate felt she needed first to gain a better understanding of her finances before jumping into the unknown: *"Sometimes women go through parts of their life where they don't know the ins and outs of their mortgage policy or their life savings or any of those things. For me, thinking about possibly making changes means understanding the part of my life that, previously, I had delegated to my husband."*

  The best way to take that leap of faith is to build a safety net for yourself. Consider how nature does this. Cliff-dwelling birds lay pear-shaped eggs so that when the eggs roll they do so in circles rather than falling off the cliff. Women also have to create safety nets, including social safety nets of new friendships. They may renew old ties to replace the social contacts they leave behind at work.

## Phase 3: Existing Betwixt and Between

**Identity Statement:** *Who am I?*
**Task:** *To get in touch with the many aspects of yourself.*
**Emotional Response:** *Fear, panic and depression.*
**Strategy:** *To take stock and repair.*
During this phase of the Vantage Process you feel like a blank business card—no title, no phone, no place, no job—a nobody. For many of you it may be the first time since you

were three years old that you have no structure in your day and a blank agenda.

You know that you are in the phase of betwixt and between because your identity as a butcher, baker, candlestick maker is taking a backseat and has not yet been replaced by a new identity. The ties to that old identity are beginning to loosen. This happens when you begin to break the mental association between what you have done and who you are. For Deanna the breakthrough was when she realized that work and working at the bank were not synonymous. There could be work and life after the bank. It is shortsighted to define yourself only in terms of your current employer. Nonetheless, you are still left wondering—Who am I? I once was . . . but now I am just Mary? Who is Mary?

A major challenge in this phase is knowing how to introduce yourself. The usual response is to still describe yourself in terms of your professional identity, your previous jobs or roles. In Deanna's case, "I am a former banker." In Laurie's case, "I am the former director of the School of Nursing." You do this because you are in a period of suspension— suspended between your old life and an uncertain future. You feel you are in "no man's land"—betwixt and between.

Deanna felt that *sabbatical* was the most appropriate term to describe the time she took to think about what she was going to do next. Sabbaticals are common in academia and are a time for recovery, renewal and for discovering new directions. It was during Laurie's and Deanna's sabbatical year that they first had the idea for this book.

But deep down, you fear that it's all over, that you're a has-been. You may feel paralyzed, stuck—not knowing in which direction to move. You may also feel desperate and find yourself retreating to things that give you comfort and make you feel safe and secure—like a chair in front of the refrigerator. Not a good option.

We understand these feelings and reactions all too well. Nobody moves from a known situation to another situation without passing through a period of uncertainty. Many of you felt as if you were jumping off a cliff. The emotional response in this phase may be fear, panic and depression.

Uncertainty is one of the most uncomfortable feelings you can experience. People often turn back in order to find the certain, the known zone again. Think of the ancient Israelite slaves when they left Egypt for the promised land. At the first hint of difficulty, they panicked and wanted to return to Egypt and a horrible life of slavery, rather than face the uncertainty of the desert and the uncertainty of their destination. Fear of uncertainty makes people act prematurely and out of panic. Even if financially or emotionally you need to start looking for a job or something to do, you must still spend some time betwixt and between.

At the very least, you should make time to articulate your dream so that you are more aware of what you want and are able to recognize opportunities when they present themselves.

If you find you need to do something to fill your days, do the projects that you have put off for so many years—paint your bedroom, finish long-forgotten, half-done projects, spend more time with friends.

Betwixt and between is a difficult phase to be in. You need to make time specifically for reflection and introspection. The strategy in this phase is to take stock and give yourself time to repair and heal.

Remember Nicole who hid out for the first couple of weeks after losing her job and her lover. Her son had also just left home. Then one morning, she woke up and thought, *"I have this time and I don't want deadlines. I worked in advertising. Advertising is a life of deadlines. I didn't want this anymore. I had to deprogram myself. I had to start feeling, really feeling. It started with slowing down."*

Nicole needed to slow down in order to take stock. This is the work of this phase in the Vantage Process. Taking stock involves considering your strengths and identifying resources (Chapters 5 and 6), removing obstacles (Chapter 7) and assessing your readiness for change (Chapter 8). This phase builds the bridge from the past to the future by taking stock of the present.

The other strategy in Phase 3 is repairing and healing. Burke told us *"For the first five years of my life, we lived on a lake in Minnesota. For the first two months after I retired from full-time work, I moved to a cabin on a lake near Washington. I returned to my roots and felt the way I had felt when I was younger."*

In coming to terms with past events you need to engage in acts of repair that heal the assaults to your identity. What parts of myself are really bruised and what can I do to make myself feel better about myself? Even if you can't find a full-time position, look for a part-time position or a volunteer position to repair your bruised ego. One woman told us how she got involved as a volunteer on a committee that validated and valued her knowledge of accounting. In her previous job, she had been told that her accounting skills were outdated.

Another form of repairing and renewing is engaging in "crop rotation." Crop rotation is a system used by farmers when they either leave the land fallow to renew and repair itself or plant a different crop that adds other nutrients to the soil. This is done to build a healthier and better future crop. When the singer Joni Mitchell felt she was burning out, she reported on television that she engaged in crop rotation—she left her songwriting and turned to painting. The important act is to take a rest from what you were doing, and develop other talents as a way of discovering yourself anew.

Some women taking time out keep themselves as busy as they had been before by transfering their energy from work to play. They go from activity to activity just to fill their appointment book. They have been trained to do this. Often, this has an anesthetizing effect where there is no time to think. If you find yourself doing this you should find a way to put "thinking" on your agenda.

Anne made an important observation about how work-oriented women react when they leave their jobs. *"The first thing you have to learn is how to relax. You are used to a routine. So when you first stop, it could be very euphoric—but I guess you have to make that jump between shocks. You've got to chill out a little. I think that, as women, we don't give ourselves permission to do just that—chill out. Why don't we play golf? Why don't we take off an afternoon to just play? I play a lot of golf now."*

Another reason you may be feeling angst at this time is that, without work, structure and routine are now absent from your life. The solution is to build routine into your day. Routine helps bring structure and gives you a sense of some control. It also helps to deal with anxiety caused by the uncertainty of not knowing where you are going and what you are going to do next. Remember, you are still in "no man's land"—betwixt and between.

Uncertainty is also a function of ambiguity. Ambiguity means that things are not clear. According to Merle Mishel, a professor of nursing at the University of North Carolina, the antidote to ambiguity is getting information.[2] This takes time, especially if it is information about yourself.

Monette tells the story of how she took time when she was in "no man's land" to gather as much information as she could about how people reconstructed their lives. *"I needed a deadline. I had to earn a living. I had only so much money that would last so long. I spent three months visiting people and asking them, 'How did you get to where you are? And why are you doing what you are doing?' I discovered that some people got there by accident. They were in the right place at the right time and took the risk at that time. When I realized that the whole universe was open to me, I asked myself, 'What do I really want to do now?' So I did take the time off but in my own way. I didn't go into my garden to think as others have done. I did tons of research. We all do it differently."*

In this phase of the process, Deanna filled her agenda with many different activities as a way of "sampling from the menu" of what had once been considered play activities, such as going to movies or galleries, exercising, playing golf. It helped her to sort out what she enjoyed, what gave her pleasure, what she did well at and what nurtured her sense of self.

Women have also told us of taking long walks in the country, finding comfort in nature. Nature heals. The calmness of the surroundings can be therapeutic in healing bruised souls. Think about how many songs have been sung about the feelings of freedom in the outdoors. Think of how many movies, how many books contain scenes of nature. Think of all the meditation tapes that capture the sound of the wind blowing, the waves of the ocean breaking, trees rustling. Think of how much better you will feel after a walk in the woods or a stroll on the beach.

Other women have found writing in journals a helpful activity. Journaling can be extremely cathartic and can help you tap into your innermost thoughts and feelings. Journaling is a way of reflecting—working through hurts.[3] You can use a journal to recount what happened, to keep a record for yourself of what you are thinking and feeling every day. In rereading journal entries you can gain greater insights into what happened to you by "hearing" yourself. The rereading may surprise even you. The nicest thing about journaling is that you are your own confidante. No one else has to know your innermost thoughts (especially not the nasty ones). You may also be surprised to see your strengths revealed on the page.

Any activity that allows you to give your mind a rest will help. When you rest your brain, you renew. Resting your brain occurs when you shut down for a while. Shutting down can come in many forms. Have you ever noticed when you have been worrying a problem to death, the solution often comes to you after a good night's sleep? Have you ever found inspiration when you were washing the kitchen floor? What we have just described are different forms of regulating yourself. In Chapter 5, Strengths, you will learn about the importance of regulation in realizing a dream.

Another strategy during this phase is to clean house. The act of repairing is like cleaning house—getting rid of the cobwebs to see what is really there at your core. Before they start a new task many women find they have to clean house. Before Laurie sits down to write she needs to tidy up. External order somehow gives her an internal sense of calmness and control.

In this phase, your task is to examine yourself. Examining does not mean tearing yourself apart. Examining doesn't mean criticizing or blaming. Examining does mean trying to understand the elements that make up your identity. Examining is a step that enables you to more deliberately decide what you want to keep, what you have to learn to live with and what you can change and reweave. The exercises in Chapter 3 can help you focus on Phase 3 and move on to Phase 4—Creating the Dream.

What is it that you really like about yourself? What things do you do that give you a good sense of yourself? In examining yourself you will probably experience a wide range of emotions. At times, you will feel hope, and at other times despair.

Marilyn moved to Greece when her husband decided to retire and to spend the winters there. She left behind her country, her reputation as a successful and well-respected physician and a proud family name that bestowed instant recognition. In her newly adopted country, she became known as Marilyn—not Marilyn the physician—not Marilyn the daughter of . . . and granddaughter of . . . What she did not leave behind was herself—all the qualities that she possessed that had made her who she was. Up until her move to Greece she could just introduce herself, and through reputation and family name, people knew a lot about her. In a new country, Marilyn had to describe herself, and she found she was forced to become reacquainted with herself.

Some women told us that what made this phase particularly difficult for them was that it was so much easier to define themselves by a job or a role. The quest now is to find the word or phrase that describes you to others. Anne, in introducing herself to us, defined herself in terms of what she enjoyed doing, with no reference to job or title.

## Phase 4: Creating the Dream

**Identity statement:** *I am becoming.*
**Task:** *To reweave threads of self.*
**Emotional Response:** *Excitement and hope.*
**Strategy:** *To explore, try on, rehearse.*

Think of Phases 3 and 4 in the Vantage Process as rebuilding your wardrobe. The task of Phase 3—Betwixt and Between—was discovering aspects of who you are. It was the stage of sorting out the closet, deciding what stays and what gets tossed. You make the decision based on knowing which clothes are dated and tired, which ones you still enjoy or that fit well and make you feel good about yourself.

The task of Phase 4 is to go shopping and try on new clothes to refurbish your wardrobe. Armed with the knowledge of what you like, you try on clothes to see how they fit. It isn't simply enough to just look, you must try on. Remember that fabulous black dress that looked terrible on the hanger but beautiful on you, or the pencil skirt that used to look great on you but may no longer suit your body? In this same way you will sift through roles and try out different activities before settling on what you want to do. The act of trying on is critical. You have to devote time to this part of the process.

Once you understand yourself better and have faced and pushed aside some of your fears and anxieties, you have cleared the path to discover your dreams. Reweaving identity helps the dreaming process and the dreaming process helps in developing identity.

So how do you go about reweaving the threads of your identity in the Vantage Years?

Identity is like breathing: You pay little attention to it unless it is threatened, assaulted or compromised in some way. Although by leaving a job or a situation you may feel you have lost part of your identity, you haven't. Your identity is not simply what job you did, but who you are. Ruthellen Josselson, in her groundbreaking book *Revising Herself,* explained "Identity in women cannot be simply named for it resides in the pattern that emerges as a woman stitches together an array of aspects of herself and her investments in others. A woman is, then, not a 'this' or a 'that' (mother, lawyer, wife, secretary, etc.) for these can only be pieces of herself. A woman is how she weaves it all into a whole, articulating herself in the world with others and simultaneously making private sense of it."[4]

Part of reweaving your identity is to think about what it is you like about yourself, how you want to spend your time, how you think of yourself and how you want others to think of you. As you learned in Chapters 2 and 3, your identity and your dreams need to be compatible, each reflecting your values. It is only when they are compatible that they can be woven together to create a meaningful life and give you a sense of wholeness.

From your dream will emanate a series of roles and these roles will become major threads in your identity. If your dream is to help others, you may have to learn different skills to assume new roles. These roles can be caregiver, teacher, student, counselor. And along with the roles, your dream will reflect values of compassion, integrity, caring. These roles and values, and the skills and competencies you have and need to develop, are the aspects that are woven to create your identity.

You have actually been through this process many times. When you became a partner, mother, worker, boss, you had to learn the job before it became an integral part of your identity. For those of you who are mothers, remember how at first you may have gone through the motions of being a mother, acting the way mothers behave, performing mothering tasks like diapering, feeding, soothing. But it might not have been until months later that you thought of yourself as a mother. Most people are unaware of the process they are going through in taking on a new role until the role becomes an integral part of who they are.

Let us consider what is involved in taking on a new role.

Any role involves a set of expectations of how to behave and is accompanied by a unique set of skills, many of which you already have, and others you will have to learn. There is usually a cognitive or thinking part to the role— how to behave in the role, when to assume the role, what to do in the role and why. There is usually some emotional investment in the role. Fatima left medicine to follow her dream of becoming a professional singer. The same qualities that made her a successful doctor—assertiveness, can-do attitude, intelligence, tenacity—are the strengths that she is now calling on to follow her new dream. She is adding to her competencies with voice training, marketing and music selection. Her identity is being rewoven into a different pattern with some new threads intertwined with the old.

There are several ways we come to learn what's involved in a role:

- **Observing others in the same role.** For those of you who have always dreamt about being a chef, you watch Julia Child or Jacques Pepin or Nigella Lawson cook on television. Some of you actually try out their recipes.
- **Shadowing a person.** Spend time in a person's milieu and observe their everyday activities. The management guru Henry Mintzberg studied the daily habits of company presidents by documenting their hour-by-hour, day-to-day activities in his book *The Nature of Managerial Work.*[5] By shadowing them, he gained insights into how they ran large corporations and talked to them about why they did what he observed them doing.
- **Apprenticing with a master.** Apprenticeship is the oldest form of learning on the job—tried-and-true.
- **Studying.** In a formal program of study to become a lawyer, nurse, doctor, teacher, you gain knowledge and skills and are socialized on how to behave. Others of you learn best by reading books including self-help books and autobiographies of famous people.
- **Imagining.** You have to visualize yourself in a role before you are actually in it. That's why writers imagine their characters—how they are dressed, where they

live. Politicians envision themselves on the podium giving the acceptance speech. Athletes picture themselves crossing the finish line. In their mind's eye, they see themselves performing the role. Imagination is an underestimated tool. It is something we can all afford and it is limitless.

- **Rehearsing.** Actors, musicians, singers rehearse their roles. Runners train for a marathon. It isn't prudent to go into something cold turkey. You come to this stage of life already having rehearsed many roles.

- **Learning and practicing new skills.** Every role has its own unique skills. Part of the task of creating a new identity is learning and acquiring these skills. Josie, a New York investment banker, was always interested in small business and women, and honed those skills and interests to become a partner in a small-business venture fund, a fund that invested in women-owned small businesses. *"It suddenly dawned on me, somehow I could help some women-owned businesses and get more involved in that area with my expertise . . . So I went to work at Women's Asset Management. Although it was short-lived it was a most interesting exercise. It was a real eye-opener for me. Out of that I decided that I really did want to try to start some women venture funds."*

- **Jumping in and doing it.** If you want to be something, then do it. Only when you have acted in the new role, can you begin to understand what it's all about and gradually incorporate the new role into your identity.

This phase is generally characterized by emotions of excitement, joy and hope, tempered with some trepidation. It is not always smooth sailing. If you are still experiencing undue fears and anxiety, this may be a warning signal that you are not yet ready for the work needed here. You may not have sufficiently attended to the tasks of the earlier phases or you may be preparing for a dream that isn't quite right.

## Phase 5: Living the Dream

**Identity statement:** *I am me.*
**Task:** *To connect.*
**Emotional Response:** *Happiness, fulfillment.*
**Strategy:** *To live it.*

Once you get to Phase 5 you have successfully made the transition. You are no longer defining yourself in terms of your job title. You now define yourself in terms of the person you are. In Phase 5 the task is to enjoy your life and feel you are living the life you want. You have connected with your authentic dream. Kevin Costner recently summed up this phase during a TV interview when he said, *"I am living the life I dreamt of."* In this phase you should feel at peace and have a sense of harmony, contentment and balance. This is not to say that you do not experience moments of doubt or dissatisfaction, but these should be transient. You will learn more about the signposts on the way to living your dream in Chapter 10.

The table on the opposite page summarizes the Vantage Process and will help you identify where you are in the process.

**THE VANTAGE PROCESS**

| | Identity Statement | Task | Emotional Responses | Strategy |
|---|---|---|---|---|
| **Phase 1: Recognizing Warning Signals** | I am my job | to recognize early signals of change | shock anger anxiety | withdraw ignore prepare |
| **Phase 2: Saying Goodbye** | I am a loser | to mourn the losses | isolation panic shock anxiety depression | withdraw reflect |
| **Phase 3: Existing Betwixt and Between** | Who am I? | to examine myself | fear panic depression | take stock repair |
| **Phase 4: Creating the Dream** | I am becoming | to reweave the self | excitement hope | explore try on rehearse |
| **Phase 5: Living the Dream** | I am ME | to connect | happiness fulfillment | live it |

## How Can I Successfully Transition Through the Vantage Process?

To successfully transition through the Vantage Process and make it to Phase 5, keep these four phrases in mind:

- It's all in how you frame it.
- Clean house before you shop for the new.
- Put yourself in the right emotional zone.
- Respect the process.

**It's all in how you frame it.** "Life is ten percent what happens to you and ninety percent how you react."[6]

How you react to an event is very much related to how you appraise it. How you appraise an event is related to how you see it, how you frame it. Whether you see a glass half empty or half full determines your reaction.

Keep reminding yourself that the Vantage Process is a transition process and transition means that you are between situations. Tania told us that when her parents immigrated from Russia to Canada they had to face the overwhelming and very difficult challenges of adjusting to a new country, but on the whole they adjusted rather well. When we asked what made the difference, Tania replied, *"It was how they framed it. They approached the move as an adventure, a time to discover new things about their new country and about themselves."*

Psychologists tell us that you can learn to frame things in a more positive way. You may believe that you are a born pessimist and that you inherited this attitude from your mother or father. Even though you may have a predisposition for pessimism, it does not mean you have to be a pessimist. You can learn to be more optimistic. You can train yourself to expect that good will prevail. If you have lost your job you can say to yourself, "I am going through a rough time now." Or you can say to yourself, "I am lousy at all jobs and that's why I fail." The optimist in you sees this situation as temporary, specific and external; whereas the pessimist frames it as stable, global and internal. In other words, the optimist in you sees this situation as a single event, nonrecurring, specific to a particular situation and caused by external factors. In contrast, the pessimist frames the situation as something that is constant—never changing—happens in all situations and is because of you, not because of the situation.[7]

**Clean house before you shop for the new.** You will be able to move from phase to phase more easily if there are fewer obstacles to deal with—if you have cleaned house. Women know there is only one way to make space for new clothes, dishes and furniture, and that is to discard the old. Obstacles to successfully transitioning through the Vantage Process are those issues that were swept under the carpet and never dealt with. They tend to raise their ugly heads during periods of transition. You may have always said, "I am a terrible public speaker and that's just me." Cleaning house means throwing out old ideas about yourself and taking steps to change your perception of yourself.

**Put yourself in the right emotional zone**. You know how difficult it is to focus and get things done when you are too depressed or too anxious. Each phase of the Vantage

Process is accompanied by strong emotions like anger, anxiety, depression, fear, joy. If you can't get yourself going because you are feeling depressed or find that you are easily distracted because you are too anxious, it will be difficult for you to focus on getting things done. You will need to develop ways of calming yourself down or motivating yourself.

By the time you've reached the Vantage Years you will have a better idea of how to put yourself in the right emotional zone. You know what activities calm you—reading a book or taking a walk or exercising. You know what motivates you—getting out of the house and doing errands, calling on a friend or taking a course. Take time to think about what you've done in stressful or depressed times of your life, then try to go through this phase one step at a time, one day at a time.

**Respect the process.** You are going to be on this journey for some time. Settle in and recognize that you can enjoy the journey—not just the destination. *Process*, by definition, requires time and takes time. You can't rush through it.

Having read this chapter you now understand the Vantage Process. You can probably say, "I am in Phase 1 (Phase 2, Phase 3 . . . ) of the Vantage Process." You may find that knowing your dream will help you to transition through the Vantage Process more quickly because your dream gives you direction and hope for the future. It is the lack of direction that often causes people to get stalled in one phase or prevents them from moving forward.

Now it is time to prepare to make your dream happen. Learning about your strengths and resources and the hurdles you face—which you will do in Chapters 5, 6 and 7—will help you on your way to Phase 4—Creating the Dream. You need this information to help you validate whether the dream you have identified is the one you actually want to pursue. If you have identified several dreams, this information may help you choose your authentic dream.

five

# STRENGTHS: YOUR BEST INVESTMENT IS YOU

VELMA WALLIS, IN HER BOOK *Two Old Women*, tells a wonderful Athabaskan Indian legend about two old women belonging to The People—a nomadic tribe of the Arctic region of Alaska.[1] We retell this story because it captures the many inner strengths of women.

During a particularly harsh winter, the council band of The People decided to leave behind two old women in the wilderness to fend for themselves because The People could no longer feed them. No one expected them to survive, including themselves.

Stunned, shocked and frightened with the turn of events, Sa', the spirited one of the two, said to Ch'idzigyaak, her more despondent friend, "We will die if we just sit here and wait to die. This would prove them right about our help-lessness." Although Ch'idzigyaak felt great despair, a small feeling of hope was sparked with these words. Within this calm and cold land, death was certain if they did nothing for themselves. "Let us die trying!" And try they did. They set about finding ways to feed, clothe and shelter themselves, drawing on their accumulated memories, knowledge and skills that they had learned from early childhood but had not used in many seasons. After killing a squirrel Ch'idzigyaak sighed in relief, "Many times I have done that, but never did I think I would have to do it again." They melted water and made broth and saved the meat for later, knowing it could be their last meal. They prepared leather bindings for their snowshoes, gathered wood to build the fire, found material to build a tent. When they finished, they beamed with pride and felt lighthearted at all they had accomplished. They had survived the first weeks.

They remembered from their childhood a narrow creek with plentiful fish and pushed themselves almost beyond endurance to locate it. Each woman, exhausted, refused to give up, knowing full well that if she did, the other one would too. Each kept the other's spirits lifted with small musings and humor. After hours of walking, they finally located the creek. Their work was not yet over for the day. With blind determination they stumbled about, gathering spruce boughs for their beds and chunks of wood for the campfire despite their stiff joints, aching limbs and swollen feet. And this is how they survived the first harsh winter.

The spring brought them little time to talk or reflect on the past as the women kept busy catching muskrats and beavers, smoke-drying them for preservation. They decided to catch more than their share because they still felt vulnerable to predators, both human and animal. They relied on long-used methods to shield themselves from being eaten by depositing the innards of fish they had caught far down the stream for the bears and using muskrat grease to repel the small insects. They were frugal, using all parts of the animals they had caught; knitting mitts and hats from the skin of rabbits, making utensils from the intestines of fish. They had mastered the art of survival and were thriving. They were prepared to face the next winter.

The People, returning to the same place where they had left the two old women the year before, were now in a more desperate state. Their gaunt faces and tattered clothing showed what had happened to them over the year. Luck had gone against them. When the remains of the two old women were not found, the chief of The People sent out a search party. To the search party's amazement, they found not only that the two old women had survived, but that they were ready to fight and defend themselves, a quality that heightened the search party's admiration.

With astonishment, the men realized that these two old women had not only survived but were in good health, while they, the strongest men in the band, were half starved. In an ironic twist, these two women shared their caches of food and warm clothing they had stored over the spring and summer months with The People.

These two women had saved the lives of The People. These two women, whom all had thought of as helpless and weak, served to inspire. The People rediscovered their own strengths that had deserted them the winter before and regained their moral compass. Never again did The People abandon their elderly. As Wallis writes, "[The People] had learned a lesson taught by two whom they came to love, care for, and respect until each died a truly happy old woman."

From reading this story and from your own life experience, you know that humans are equipped for survival and growth. We call upon our strengths not only to survive but also to build a meaningful life. By the time you have reached the Vantage Years, you have accumulated many wonderful and useful strengths and skills. In moving towards realizing your dreams, you will be relying on these strengths and discovering new ones.

You build strengths through successes, mistakes and so-called failures. By this stage in life, you realize that mistakes are not all negative. Mistakes prepare you for the next chance, the next opportunity, the next stage in life. The best investment you have made has been in yourself, in building your strengths. Now is the time to capitalize on these as you move forward.

In this chapter you will learn the answers to these questions:

- What are strengths and why is it necessary to know them?
- How do I identify and assess my strengths?
- What strengths do I need to realize my dream?
- How can I work on my strengths to realize my dream?

## What Are Strengths and Why Is It Necessary to Know Them?

Montaigne wrote of a woman who lifted a calf every day and was still able to lift it as it grew to be a cow.[2] This woman achieved the "impossible" because she worked on her strengths day by day and because she believed she could do it. This woman called on her physical and mental powers to lift the cow.

As you get older, your diminishing physical strength is more than offset by your accumulated mental, social, emotional and moral strengths. Strengths are those special qualities that in their combination and methods of expression give you your unique signature—your "strength DNA." You have accumulated the ABCs of strengths. These include: A for attitude (ways of thinking); B for building blocks (valuable qualities); and C for competencies (skills). Think of strengths as your ABCs—the best qualities within you. (See the table on p. 122.)

Genevieve has always lived with a spirited attitude toward life: *"The choices I made in my youth, I made spontaneously. I was visiting friends and there was a bean crock made of pottery. I fell in love with the pot and decided to be a potter. I became a potter. When I decided to go back to library school, that decision was neither impulsive nor emotional. It was very rational. At this age I feel the finiteness of things. I feel I want to be a little bit crazy again."*

Among the building blocks on which Melanie has called are the invaluable qualities of courage and confidence: *"Basically I have the belief that I can do it, I have what it takes. I have the guts to do this. It's going to work out. I have to believe in myself."*

Helene told us, *"I remember sitting in the car in front of the kids' ballet school waiting to pick them up and reading my school notes on the steering wheel so I could maximize the use of my time."* A competency that many women have is the ability to multitask.

Women often fail to appreciate the worth of their inner strengths. How often have you heard a woman discount or devalue a compliment about one of her strengths—"You are such a capable homemaker." Response (with a wave of the hand and a lowering of the eyes): "Tsch, it's nothing."

Women also fail to realize that their strengths are transferable from one situation to another seemingly unconnected situation—from the personal to the work environment, for example. As Kathleen Brown, former managing director of Goldman Sachs and a one-time California state treasurer, said: "The skills I learned in playgroups, trust me, I use in politics and in the boardroom."[3]

Take such skills as multitasking, organizing, going with the flow, supervising, negotiating, planning and so on. Many women are experts at them. When Deanna taught a supervisory training course for women, most of the attendees had been out of the workforce for many years. They were nervous and lacked confidence. They did not believe they could manage or supervise others. But they came to realize that many of the skills that they had developed at home could be used in a work environment. A mother of six children didn't think of her skills as "system design" skills. Yet these were the very skills she employed when she gave each of her children their own laundry basket to be delivered to the washing machine. She then did the laundry and returned the clean clothes to each child's basket for pick-up. This saved her endless hours of picking up and sorting laundry. Imagine, each child actually wore his or her own socks! Here is a woman who was an efficiency expert, who had taken this strength for granted and was unaware of its significance.

Women often focus on their weaknesses rather than on their strengths. This is hardly surprising given our over-critical society in which we spend much of our time looking for deficiencies, looking for what is missing rather than for what is there. This focus is so much a part of our culture that when students bring home a report card with a bad grade along with their good grades—a D or F along with As, Bs or Cs—many parents will spend most of the time discussing the Ds or Fs.[4]

Focusing on deficiencies, on what is missing, on what you don't have or comparing yourself to another person whom you consider more successful, can be paralyzing and inevitably leads to a sense of inertia and despair—an "I can't do it" attitude. It is a sure-fire way of putting a very short expiry date on a dream. Strengths, on the other hand, serve to anchor and buoy you up. Your outlook on events affects how you behave, and how you behave affects how you think and feel. In fact, research has shown that when people focus on their strengths, they feel better about themselves and are more likely to take charge of their life.[5, 6]

## How Do I Identify and Assess My Strengths?

Think of strengths as the wide range of building materials that you have acquired through a lifetime of experience, practice and learning. These are the materials that you are now going to use to create and fulfill your dream. Different dreams require different strengths.

The most efficient and effective way to get started on your dream is to build upon qualities you already have. None of you would have gotten to this phase of your life without developing a large basket of strengths and skills. It is your task now to look inside your basket and to appreciate how you can use your existing strengths to achieve your dream.

When you have assessed your strengths, you will know which you can use to implement your dream and which others you need to develop. Naming or labeling makes strengths real, gives them value and helps you to understand them better. When you name a strength you are making the invisible visible, the implicit explicit, both to yourself and to others. If you want the dream to happen, you can't rely on serendipity or chance. You have to make it happen.

We have created an inventory of strengths that are critical for dreaming (see the ABCs of Strengths on the next page). You will be referring to this list to complete the exercises in this chapter.

While we recognize and acknowledge that everyone has weaknesses or deficiencies, we focus on capitalizing and strengthening existing attitudes, building blocks and competencies. You have to be aware of your weaknesses and alert to how these may sabotage, limit and undermine your efforts to move forward. One important strength is learning to manage them.

Each of the strengths in the table is present in every person, but in varying degrees. A particular strength may vary depending on what you are doing and what is important to you at a given time. Some of you will be more tenacious than others and more tenacious in some activities than in others. Laurie can cook for hours but has little patience for reading a business plan. Deanna's patience for cooking is limited to minutes, but she can spend hours analyzing a business plan. We are both tenacious but our tenacity varies according to our interests. (Lucky for us that we had the same level of tenacity while writing this book.)

## THE ABCs OF STRENGTHS

| Attitude | Building Blocks | Competencies |
|---|---|---|
| Altruistic | Accountable | Communicator |
| Caring | Adaptable | Decision-maker |
| Collaborative | Assertive | Implementer |
| Competitive | Charismatic | Leader |
| Compassionate | Charming | Multitasker |
| Cooperative | Chutzpah | Navigation skills |
| Easygoing | Committed | Negotiator |
| Enthusiastic | Common Sense | Organizer |
| Forgiving | Confident | Planner |
| Generous | Courageous | Problem solver |
| Good-natured | Creative | Time manager |
| Grateful | Curious | |
| Helpful | Disciplined | |
| Hopeful | Educated | |
| Humble | Emotional IQ | |
| Independent | Endurance | |
| Joyful | Energetic | |
| Open | Goodness-of-fit | |
| Optimistic | Hardiness | |
| Positive | Honest | |
| Proud | Humorous | |
| Spirited | Loyal | |
| Warm | Patient | |
| | Physical attractiveness | |
| | Polite | |
| | Regulation | |
| | Resiliency | |
| | Resourceful | |
| | Respectful | |
| | Risk-taker | |
| | Self-accepting | |
| | Self-aware | |
| | Self-efficacy | |
| | Sociable | |
| | Spiritual | |
| | Timing | |
| | Tenacious | |

The inventory in the ABCs of Strengths is by no means exhaustive. In fact, we would encourage you to add to this list as you become aware of your own strengths. You will have the opportunity to do this when you complete the exercises that develop your personal inventory of strengths.

---

## Exercise: Getting in Touch With Your Strengths
(Time to complete: 30 minutes–two days)

Compile a list of what you see as your strengths. If you need help getting in touch with your strengths, here are three options from which to choose. You can elect to do one, two or all three.

*Option 1.* Borrow from the ABCs of Strengths, and jot down in your notebook the ones that apply to you.

*Option 2.* Keep a diary for two days to identify your strengths. Record situations, good and bad, and how you handled them. Take time to note incidents as they happen rather than waiting to remember them at the end of the day. Reread your notes and highlight the words or phrases that describe your strengths.

*Option 3.* Ask yourself the following questions:

"What do I do well in my work? In my personal life?"

"What do other people tell me that I do well?"

Write the answers out and then highlight the words or phrases that describe your strengths.

Whichever option you use, draw up an inventory of your strengths.

---

## What Strengths Do I Need to Realize My Dream?

We have selected nine strengths from the ABCs of Strengths, which we believe are useful for all dreams.

S—Self-acceptance
T—Tenacity
R—Regulation
E—Efficacy
N—Navigational skills
G—Goodness-of-fit
T—Timing
H—Humor
S—Spiritedness

**Self-acceptance.** With the Vantage Years, you come to understand your strengths, and have learned to accept and compensate for the qualities that are more difficult to change. Moreover, you have come to understand what matters to you and how to act to protect and promote yourself. This is self-acceptance and should not be confused with self-aggrandizement. Those who genuinely have a good sense of themselves, in fact, tend to be humble and modest. They don't boast. What struck us about the women we interviewed was their modesty and humility in describing their achievements. Most of these women had a level of self-acceptance despite being aware of their shortcomings. Self-acceptance enables you to select a realistic dream.

**Tenacity.** Other words related to tenacity are *persistence, perseverance, stick-to-it-iveness.* Tenacity is the ability to stay with a problem or an interest. This strength is a major determinant in realizing a dream. You might be detoured and deterred by circumstance but it is those who pick themselves up, dust themselves off and get back on track who have the best chance of achieving their dream.

Lettie, whose story you heard in Chapter 1, elevates tenacity to new heights. It took her almost thirty years to realize her teenage calling to become an Anglican priest, all the while finding alternative routes to realizing her dream. Lettie illustrates the difference between tenacity and stubbornness.

Trying to get to the other side of a brick wall by beating your head repeatedly against it is stubbornness. Finding a way around it is tenacity. The words you hear a tenacious person say are: "How can I do this?" "How can I make this happen?" You never hear them say, "It is impossible."

**Regulation of self.** Through self-regulation we have learned to control and modulate our needs, emotions, thoughts and feelings and how we manage stress. Self-regulation is about how attuned we are to the signals of our mind and body. We are all born with signaling mechanisms to protect us. These signals tell us how much to eat and when to stop, when to sleep and when to get up, what calms us and what upsets us.

One of the first challenges that newborns face is how to soothe themselves when they experience feelings of discomfort. Initially they rely on good parents to figure out why they are uncomfortable. Parents try many things to soothe crying infants—they rock them, change them, feed them and carry them about. With time infants learn the basic techniques of self-soothing. Finding their thumb is a major milestone both in their lives and in their sleepless parents' lives. As adults you have found many "thumbs" to use. Your ability to manage your behavior, thoughts and emotions, such as not getting angry when it serves little purpose, is a major strength and will be called on to achieve your dream.

When Sa' and Ch'idzigyaak, the two old Indian women, saved some of the squirrel meat to eat later or when they rested, they were practicing self-regulation. Athletes and performers need to be excellent self-regulators. They need to know just how far to push their bodies. Araceli Segarra, who climbed Mount Everest, understood how to self-regulate to realize her dream when she said, "People think I am strong and can run a marathon, but I can't. I just go slowly."[7]

You have also learned by now how to self-regulate even if you have not recognized this behavior as a strength nor called it by this name. At twenty you may have had the stamina and the desire to party until dawn; at forty-five you pace yourself differently so that you can function at maximum capacity. At twenty you may have flown off the handle when upset; at forty-five you have learned ways to keep your temper under control. You will need to call upon your skills of self-regulation when realizing dreams as you deal with disappointments, frustrations and "bumps in the road."

Without self-regulation you will not be sufficiently resilient to deal with the challenges that these years will bring. Your resiliency is what brought you to these years and resiliency will help you realize your dream.

**Efficacy.** Self-efficacy is the degree to which you are able to change or fix a situation. Those with a "can do" attitude have a high degree of self-efficacy.[8] If you believe that you are going to be able to do something or be able to change, then the odds tip in your favor.

When you start, you select something that you know you can excel at. Evelyn, who lives in London, was initially driven to get services for her son with special needs. She developed a "can do" attitude with each successive victory she won over the educational and social authorities in securing the best services for her son. She has since used her knowledge and skills to advocate for other parents in similar situations.

Efficacious people don't have unrealistic expectations that everything will go smoothly, but they do believe that they can do it. A good mantra to keep in mind is, "What I can't do, I don't do. What I can do, I do." As Madame C.J. Walker, the African-American cosmetics tycoon and philanthropist said, "I got my start by giving myself a start."

**Navigational skills** is the combination of strengths that help you move through familiar and unfamiliar terrain on your way to realizing your dreams. Women in their everyday lives have to be excellent multitaskers, organizers, problem solvers and planners. Think of the many decisions and options you consider as you navigate the aisles of the grocery store. You are weighing the likes and dislikes of each family member, thinking of different menu options, taking advantage of specials and incorporating them into your menu, considering freshness of produce, nutritional values and best-before dates, comparing prices and so on. Sociologists call this the invisible work of women. This strength will help you enormously as you identify and then implement the stages of your dream. Sa' and Ch'idzigyaak's navigational skills speak for themselves. These two women survived where the strongest men were half-starved.

**Goodness-of-fit,** a term coined by psychiatrists Stella Chess and Alexander Thomas, refers to how well your temperament and skills fit with the demands of specific environments.[9] Being strong in this area helps you to select those situations in which you will do well. Goodness-of-fit requires the ability to size up a situation and to determine whether it is good for you or not. Sa' and Ch'idzigyaak survived because of their stubbornness and intimate knowledge of their environment.

Goodness-of-fit requires a healthy degree of self-knowledge. People who have mastered a goodness-of-fit with different environments are often the people we say have "street smarts." This is a major strength because finding your dream will depend upon recognizing and creating a good fit.

Goodness-of-fit requires a form of acquired intelligence, popularly known as emotional intelligence. Daniel Goleman, in his bestselling books on emotional intelligence (which he calls EQ), writes about what is required to achieve a good fit between yourself and your environment.[10, 11] A measure of self-awareness, empathy for others, self-discipline are but some of the qualities that go into EQ. The good news is that EQ can be constantly developed and strengthened throughout your life. Natalie has a favorite quote that sums up the importance of knowing how to deal with a situation that doesn't fit or feel right: *"When the horse is dead, get off."*

**Timing.** A good sense of timing is a definite strength for dreaming. As in the card game poker, the skill is in knowing when to hold them and when to fold them.

But the old adage that "timing is everything" is only partially true. Being at the "right place at the right time" is also only partially true. Both of these statements imply that you have little control. But that's not true. Good timing also comes with planning and being prepared. Good timing involves knowing where to be, reading environmental cues, pacing yourself accordingly, waiting for the moment that will maximize your efforts. If you develop a greater sensitivity to yourself and your environment, you will find you will have a better sense of timing.

**Humor.** A sense of humor is an undervalued but critical building block to dreaming and to living well. Humor is a well-known way of coping and relieving stress. Humor and laughter mitigate hurts, divert attention, bring lightness to potentially overwhelming and oppressive situations, relieve tension and allow for healing. It's a good thing to see the humor in the situation and in so doing open yourself up to new possibilities.

The road to realizing a dream is never direct or smooth. That's what adds a new and interesting dimension to the dream. At this stage of life, you might have learned the pleasure of not taking yourself or life too seriously. Elaine, with a sense of humor and a twinkle in her eye, told us about how she dealt with breast cancer: *"If I'm going to go through this, I'm going to have fun. So I went with a different friend to radiation every day and we went to lunch. It got so that people called me and said, 'Could we come, too?' I thought I was going to have to charge money."*

**Spiritedness.** Being spirited involves being vigorous, coura-geous, creative, taking measured risk and trying out new things. It does not mean being reckless. Being spirited means having the courage to face difficulty without fear, hav-ing confidence in your dreams and taking charge. Spirited people look at change and challenge as an opportunity not as an obstacle. If you view this period of life positively, you will have increased your chances of realizing your dream. It is this kind of attitude that fuels your spirit and gives you zest.

Sa' and Ch'idzigyaak embody the ultimate in spiritedness.

---

### Exercise: Assessing Your Strengths for Dreaming
(Time to complete: 60 minutes)

In this exercise, you will assess how well each of the nine strengths for dreaming is working for you.

*Step 1:* On a page in your notebook, place the nine strengths for dreaming in the left-hand column (see oppo-site for example).

*Step 2:* Assess each strength according to how well it works for you or whether it needs attention. For example, you may note that you start projects but tend to run out of steam. While tenacity may be a strength, it obviously needs attention. You can simply place a check mark in the appro-priate box or write yourself a note.

**EXAMPLE: ASSESSING STRENGTHS**

| | Working Well | Needs Attention |
|---|---|---|
| S—Self Acceptance | I generally feel good about myself | _____ |
| T—Tenacity | I stick with and finish most projects | I don't recognize when I should give up |
| R—Regulation | _____ | I should take a short nap every afternoon because I run out of steam |
| E—Efficacy | _____ | I always second-guess myself because I'm not sure I can do it |
| N—Navigational Skills | I know how to plan and can usually follow through | _____ |
| G—Goodness-of-Fit | I know that I like to take my time and I know I don't work well in a fast-paced environment | _____ |
| T—Timing | _____ | I often act prematurely |
| H—Humor | I can always see the humor in a difficult situation | _____ |
| S—Spiritedness | I'm always ready for the next adventure | Sometimes I get carried away |

## How Can I Work on My Strengths to Realize My Dream?

If you noted that any of the strengths for dreaming needed attention or if you decided to develop any of your own strengths, there are four basic ways to do this:

- Educate yourself
- Observe others
- Be coached
- Practice

**Educate yourself.** To gain knowledge about a skill, you study, take courses, read, gather information. This technique is most often used to build competencies like planning, organization and time management.

**Observe others.** Almost everything you know has been acquired, to some extent, by observing others and then trying it out yourself. Cooking and decorating shows are built on observational learning. People learn many professions and trades by observing a master physician, engineer, lawyer, nurse, plumber, craftsperson. Donna, an artist, believed she had a special gift for healing others. She connected with and then observed other healers as a way of learning this art.

**Be coached.** Anyone that you trust can be your coach—sister, brother, friend, neighbor, colleague. One of the fastest growing professions is that of the personal coach who helps you to develop a new attitude, building block or competency. A personal coach is usually somebody with specific expertise, who observes you in different situations, points out what you do well, analyzes your particular skills or strengths and alerts you to how others see and react to you.

**Practice.** Practice is what perfects our building blocks and competencies. You learn through trial and error, by trying things out and correcting yourself. Even attitudes such as optimism, positive perspective, hopefulness can be learned by becoming aware of negative thinking, deliberately changing this way of thinking and then practicing it until the new attitude replaces the old and becomes a new way of thinking. Melanie explained how she changed her attitude: *"When you're starting to make a change, you have to have a fundamental belief in yourself. 'Okay, I've got what it takes. I can do this . . .' I keep repeating this over and over again. Nobody said this is easy. I just have to keep at it."*

By the end of this chapter you will have made an inventory of your strengths and have learned about the strengths that will help you realize your dreams. You will also know which strengths require work and you will be thinking about how to improve them. In addition to these strengths, you will need resources to help you along the way. These resources and how to access and use them are described and discussed in the next chapter.

six

# RESOURCES: TAKING STOCK
# AND TAKING CHARGE

*"I'M NOT AFRAID OF DYING, I'm afraid of getting old. I am afraid of becoming dependent and losing my self-sufficiency,"* Nicole says.

Naomi told us, *"I just said to myself: 'Okay. I'm scared, I'm nervous.' I thought, 'I don't have enough money to retire.' We are all afraid we're going to be bag ladies. So I was afraid about finances. I was afraid about my health. I was afraid about what I was going to do when I left my job. I was afraid about all of these things. I just felt the fear. I felt the discomfort. As each day passed, I started to do things that I liked and even things that I had never enjoyed—like exercise. I even got to like doing that."*

Heidi confided, *"I worry about growing old and alone."*

The women we interviewed gave voice to what most Vantage Women worry about: finding themselves unwell, poor and alone, not having enough money to enjoy a reasonable lifestyle, not having enough to do to fill their time or that their time will be filled with activities that have little meaning for them. These worries can be major inhibitors to getting in touch with your dreams. These worries can stop you in your tracks. You may find yourself saying, I want to— BUT my health won't permit it—BUT I can't afford to—BUT I can't do it by myself—BUT I can't learn that—BUT I don't have the time.

Along with your inner strengths, you have other primary resources to call on: health, finance and relationships are primary resources. Before you can create the road map to your dreams, you need to get a handle on how sound your resource base is.

Resources fuel your life so you can do what you want to do. Shummy, at age eighty-one, is able to live the life of her dreams. She is healthy and financially secure, with many people in her life who care about her and about whom she cares. In a space of two months, she flew from her home in Buenos Aires to Victoria, British Columbia, to help plant her son's garden, visited her daughter in Toronto, took her grandchildren on a visit to Washington, D.C., and spent a month in her birth city of London, England.

Worries and concerns about any of your resources can sap your energy, leaving you physically, emotionally and mentally drained. These worries can be so overwhelming and all-consuming that they can divert you from following your dreams. Only when you take charge and have some measure of control can you mitigate or alleviate the worry and move forward with your life.

When you are young you tend to pay little attention to these primary resources. They are just there, taken for granted. You may even abuse them. Gwen: *"I still consider myself reasonably energetic, even though I can't do all that I used to do when I was in my thirties. I used to stay up . . . I could be working all night long. Not only do I not want to do that anymore, I can't physically take it anymore."*

This chapter does not focus on specific ways to solve your health, financial and relationship concerns. There are many books, articles and websites devoted to health, diet, exercise, menopause, meditation, yoga, investing for retirement, managing your finances, choosing careers, improving your relationships, managing your time and so on. Many of these are excellent sources of information that show you how to build a healthier, more financially secure, more connected and better balanced you. This chapter focuses on taking stock of and taking charge of these resources and turning them to your advantage.

At the end of this chapter you will find a sampling of informative books and websites that reflect today's best practices.

In this chapter you are going to learn more about:

- Taking stock and taking charge of your health, finances and relationships.
- The ten-minute Resource Checkup.

## Taking Stock and Taking Charge of Your Health, Finances and Relationships

You need to take stock of your health, finances and relationships to determine how sound your resource base is. Then you must discover how much of each resource you require to make you comfortable.

Your measure of comfort with these resources is related to how you feel about them, your expectations and what resources you need in order to achieve your dream. For example, there are many people with chronic physical conditions, such as diabetes, who have a full life and who see themselves as healthy, whereas some health professionals might see them as unwell. Some people who live with diabetes feel they can do anything, while others may feel more limited in what they can do.

Many people live on incomes they judge to be more than adequate to meet their needs, while others might consider these people's assets and income inadequate. Sound financial control and management of your earnings, savings, spending, debt and investing determine how you feel about your financial state—not the actual dollar amount that you earn or the assets you own.

In the table Resource Issues for Vantage Women (next page), we have identified issues that women in their forties, fifties, sixties, seventies and beyond may encounter. You have your own issues that come to the forefront and recede periodically. How these are experienced is subjective, very much your own. You need to identify which ones are of concern, accept those that you cannot change and mitigate as much as possible their negative effects on your life. You need to take charge so that you can get on with creating your dreams.

**Health.** Health is already one of the most written-about topics and will only become more compelling as boomers age. Although women in their early years are concerned about health, it is in the Vantage Years that good health can no longer be taken for granted. For many women their

## RESOURCE ISSUES FOR VANTAGE WOMEN

| | Health | Finance | Relationships |
|---|---|---|---|
| Forties | • Perimenopausal symptoms<br>• Weight gain<br>• Stress | • Paying bills<br>• Buying a house<br>• Children's education and upbringing | • Marital problems<br>• Adolescent children<br>• Community service |
| Fifties and Sixties | • Menopausal symptoms<br>• Sleep cycle change<br>• Weight gain<br>• Changes in appearance<br>• Dips in energy<br>• Depression<br>• Increased risk of disease<br>• Stress | • Retirement savings<br>• Investment opportunities<br>• Mortgage payments<br>• Health-care costs<br>• University costs<br>• Diminished earnings | • Loneliness<br>• Launching children<br>• Caring for aging, frail parents |
| Seventies and Beyond | • Decreased muscle strength and mobility<br>• Decreased sensory functions<br>• Increased risk of disease and injury<br>• Shortened sleep cycles<br>• Depression<br>• Stress | • Enough money<br>• Portfolio risk<br>• Health-care costs<br>• Diminished earnings | • Loneliness<br>• Difficulty building and expanding social network<br>• Illnesses, death<br>• Grandchildren |

health is a major concern, so much so that researchers have shown that women report more health concerns and are more worried about their health than are men.[1] Women have more chronic health problems than men. During the Vantage Years, women become increasingly concerned about preventing conditions that may lead to early death and mitigating chronic conditions such as cancer, heart disease, stroke and diabetes.[2]

Again, health is a subjective state that only you can determine. Nobody can tell you how healthy you feel. How healthy you feel, irrespective of how healthy you actually are, will affect the type of dreams you entertain. We know many women who have had back surgery—some have taken to their beds while others have gone hiking or biking.

You need to think of health as broader than disease control. Think of your health in terms of how well you function, how satisfied you are with your life, the level to which you are able to rally or recover from illness or assaults, how balanced and content you feel. In short, health is the degree to which you approach life with grace, vigor and energy, regardless of the number of aches and pains from which you suffer.

Although everyone ages, you may be able to manage the effects of aging by taking control of your health. Some losses can be prevented and others slowed, depending primarily upon lifestyle choices and your attitude. Diet, exercise, stress levels, exposure to sun, alcohol, tobacco and drugs play important roles in how well you age. Your attitude about your life affects the choices you make. Aging is inevitable— but feeling old and infirm is not.

During the Vantage Years, you need to spend more time and attention to prevent deterioration. You may suddenly become more concerned with your nutrition and exercise regimes, not only for their aesthetic benefits but also for their health benefits. You may stay out of the sun to prevent melanomas and wrinkles and take vitamins to raise your energy level. Feeling good widens the realm of possibilities of dreams. It is hard to dream unless you feel healthy. Genevieve sums up the change in her health: *"One of the things that became clear was that my energy level is not as high as it used to be. I'm not sleeping as well. There is a medical problem that hasn't been dealt with. My body feels like it's shutting down. Last year, I was sick for six weeks but they couldn't find anything wrong except that I was completely burnt out. I don't know how my health will limit what I want to do next."*

In addition to any aches and pains and prior conditions, all women have to deal with menopause. Some menopausal symptoms can be a part of a woman's life for up to ten years. Women experience the effects of menopause and the accompanying symptoms, both physiological and psychological. Hot flashes, night sweats, sleep disturbances, dry skin, hair thinning, redistribution of fat, weight gain, lapses in memory and attention, mood swings, depression—all serve as wake-up calls that you are aging. Do not minimize or sweep under the carpet the need to attend to your symptoms or concerns. The good news is that for most women, menopause unfolds over years, which allows both the body and psyche to adapt and accommodate. Menopause is a significant experience for all women, even for those with mild symptoms. It is a milestone in life, just as puberty was.

Much has been written about how to look and feel good regardless of your age and health. You know what it takes to promote your health and reduce your risks of disease—most of us learned the fundamentals in our health-education classes back in elementary school. What Laurie taught children in her first job as a school nurse in the late sixties, still applies today: Feeling and looking good depends on what you eat (food and vitamins), what and how much you drink, how much you exercise, how much you sleep, what risk-taking behaviors you choose to engage in and the quality of your relationships. What is different from what you learned as a child and what you need to know as Vantage Women is that your requirements for specific food, water, sleep, physical and mental activity and so forth have changed over the years.

The current wisdom is based on the latest scientific discoveries: fish, low-fat milk, fresh vegetables, broccoli, fruit, blueberries, almonds, olive oil, whole grains, red wine, tofu are in; white sugar and bleached white flour are out. Calcium, Vitamin E, D, B12, flaxseed and soy are in. Weight training, walking, Pilates and yoga are in, and jogging is out. Sleep is in, all-night partying is out. Sunscreen is in, tanning is out. Smoking is out. The debate about the risks of hormone replacement therapy (HRT) is very much in.

Fifty years ago we all were unaware of the deleterious effects of stress. Today stress is a popular topic of discussion. People say, "I am so stressed out," "The stress is killing me." These sentiments have found support in the research literature. Stress is considered a killer today because it raises cortisol levels (a stress-related hormone) and suppresses the immune system, which heightens the risk of disease.

Scientists, in looking at ways to mitigate stress, have discovered the importance of personality and relationships.

Optimism and supportive relationships are in; loneliness, isolation, negativity are out. Controlling stress is very important to your well-being. It is the support of friends that will make you feel validated, loved and understood. Such support helps you cope with stress, keeping you from becoming overwhelmed by life's challenges. Women tend to have larger networks of friends and family members from which to elicit support and they call upon these people more readily than men do. Many people have found ways to mitigate stress through exercise, yoga, meditation and getting in touch with their inner selves.

At the end of this chapter you will find an exercise— The Resource Checkup—which asks you to take stock of your health and other resources. Take a few minutes now to reflect on the following questions about your health so that when you come to the Resource Checkup you will have a good idea of those areas of health that are working for you and those that need attention.

- Do I consider myself healthy? If yes, why? If no, why not?
- Do I get regular checkups (physicals, pap smears, mammograms)?
- How healthy is my diet? Do I get a balanced amount of fruit, vegetables, carbs, protein, calcium and so on?
- Am I a healthy weight? Does my weight fall within the 19–24 range on the Body Mass Index for my age?
- Do I get enough exercise? Do I do aerobic exercise— walk, run? Are my muscles toned?
- Do I get enough sleep? Do I sleep seven to nine hours most nights?

- Do I have specific ailments or conditions?
- Are my prevailing ailments under control?
- How is my mood? Do I feel depressed, anxious?
- Is the stress in my life under control?

**Finance.** Finance is the management of your personal assets, liabilities, income, spending and savings measured in dollars and cents. Don't let anyone mislead you into thinking that *money* is a dirty word. It most certainly is not. Money enables you to maintain or improve your quality of life.

Understanding your finances is critical not only to your future but to your sense of freedom—the freedom to feel safe and secure and to do things you want to do without having to be preoccupied about money. The best way to take charge of your money is to budget, manage, save and invest it. Regardless of the amount of money involved, taking charge and control over your finances frees you to dream.

Freedom is a cherished commodity for Vantage Women—the freedom to do what you want regardless of your actual wealth. Wealth, like health, is relative and is personally defined by whether you have enough money to do the things you want to do. Your financial health is not determined by how much you actually earn but by how much you spend relative to how much you earn. Molly, a single woman, lived for thirty years on a very small pension after having been a research scientist. Her dream was to write, learn woodworking and travel. To live her dream, she reduced her spending considerably while still maintaining her lifestyle, but with a difference. She shopped in secondhand stores, no longer bought books but borrowed them from the library, traveled and stayed in hostels, cooked everything for herself and made all her gifts. Adair has a dream to travel but cannot work enough to earn the money to do so. To support her dream, she boards students in her house.

Why is finance of acute concern for women?

Many women have to deal with the quadruple whammy of longevity, living alone, lower income and having less control over their finances. Although both sexes are now living longer, women are still living approximately five years longer than men. Women also find themselves alone because of divorce or early widowhood. Women have also earned less throughout their working lives, hence have lower pensions and lower savings. Traditionally women have been financially less involved and less aggressive with their own money, often leaving financial concerns to others. Many women lack confidence in their knowledge about money management and tend to be less aggressive in their investments.

What nutrition, exercise and sleep was to managing your physical health, earning, saving, spending and investing are to managing your financial health. If you find you do not have enough money, the usual response is to try to earn more. While that might be one solution, we can't tell you how to do that. What we can advise is that financial strength is less about earnings and more about the *balance* among earnings, savings, spending and investing.

The best advice about savings is still to pay yourself first. If you do not put away the savings right at the beginning of the week or immediately from your paycheck, you are less likely to save. Another form of savings is to protect yourself by having insurance (life, health, disability, car and house). This is particularly important for self-employed women or

women without partners. Their entire livelihood is jeopard-
ized if they become sick or disabled.

Paying off your mortgage, car loan, credit-card debt are
in. Overextending yourself is out. Updating your will, assign-
ing power of attorney, keeping your important papers in order
are in. Leaving your estate in disarray is out. Saving for
retirement is in. Even in the Vantage Years it is not too late.

There are only two ways to get rich: One is to earn a lot
of money and the other is to reduce your needs. Both scenarios demand that you budget your expenses and keep your
debt manageable. We teach children to manage their
allowance—if they spend all their money on candy today,
they won't have money for that special toy tomorrow.

There will always be surprise expenses. Today the
biggest surprise expense is KIPPERS (Kids in Parents'
Pockets Eroding Retirement Savings). A British study found
that adult children in their thirties and forties were still getting financial help from their parents. Twenty-five percent
received help with cars, 25 percent with vacations; 30 percent with homes.[3] You have to beware of KIPPERS.

The issue is not how to make lots of money, but how to
get what you need to fulfill your dreams with the money you
have. We've heard it said that the quickest way to double
your money is to fold it and put it back into your pocket.[4]
That is not the best investment strategy. Depending upon
your risk tolerance, age and needs, there is a wide range of
investment possibilities available: bank deposits, certificates
of deposit, money-market instruments, fixed-rate securi-
ties, bonds and stock. There are financial institutions and
consultants who can advise you, but you should become
intimately involved in managing your money and insuring

that you have enough diversification in your portfolio to protect yourself and your future dreams.

Reflect on the following questions about your financial situation. This will prepare you for the Resource Checkup.

- How much money do I spend today? How much money do I need to spend?
- Do I have enough money to retire or to live without working?
- What lifestyle choices do I have to make to live within my means?
- Do I have a good balance between saving for myself, saving for a rainy day, saving for retirement, and insuring myself for disability, death or other untoward circumstances?
- Do I budget my expenses? How well do I follow my budget?
- Do I have a diversified portfolio—a balance between equity (stocks) and fixed-term investments, (bonds, bank deposits); and between low-risk and high-risk investments?
- Do I have enough money to realize my dream?
- Do I need my own money to realize my dream?
- How can I earn or borrow the funds to make my dream a reality?

**Relationships.** Your relationships play a central role in realizing your dreams. Those with whom you have relationships include all the people who are significant in your life such as your partner, children, parents, siblings, relatives, friends, social acquaintances, colleagues and so on. In short, anybody who touches your life and contributes to its quality is considered part of your network.

At each step of creating and living your dream you need people. No one expects you to do it alone. There is an old saying that when you see a turtle sitting on a fence post, you may not know how it got there but you can be darn sure it got help.[5]

You might call on people to help you figure things out, create your dreams, assess your strengths and resources, overcome the obstacles, create the road map—and to just be there. You need a cheering section in the stands and someone to prevent you from falling when you teeter. You need people to supplement your skill set. You need people to spur you on. You need people to lend a helpful hand and an empathetic ear. Some may need a small support group comprising a few people and others may need a larger network.

Sibyelle told us how she relies on her children for advice, support and encouragement. *"Slowly things came together after my separation and I was able to manage. I am encouraged by my children. I get lots of support from my children . . . and I talk to my children a lot about decisions and about my life. They are all very down-to-earth and sensitive and simple people. So I find that helps me."*

Genevieve told us how her brother has become her mentor at this stage in her life. *"I call him my mentor . . . my brother was laid off twice in his fifties. Although he lives in Dublin right now, he calls me once a week, and because he's gone through what I'm going through, he's just amazing. He just listens. He knows when to shut up."*

If you are to succeed and fulfill your dreams you need to understand how your personal relationships affect you. You need to gain insight into the nature of your network and learn to call upon members of your network for the right type of support. You need to identify who makes you feel valued, loved, esteemed, nurtured and gives you the help that you need. It's all about having the right person, for the right task, at the right time.

Joy told us about the role her husband played in supporting her development. *"My husband thought that there was nothing I couldn't do. I would accomplish some small thing and he would say: 'Well, what are you going to do next?' He thought I could do it and I didn't want to disappoint him."*

Angie said, *"I left a company I was with and sent out an e-mail to a network of women I know, just saying, 'I'm leaving.' And within a week, I got a call from one of them and she said, 'Look, I have this job. Are you interested?' I didn't even have to go out and search. She drew me in."*

People who are supportive are people you can count on, even when they don't always tell you what you want to hear. They are good reality checks without being critical or undermining your self-confidence. They have the uncanny knack of listening to you and hearing what you are feeling and thinking, not simply what you are saying. Keeping supportive people around you is critical to getting in touch with your dreams. It is often someone else who really hears what you have said, who interprets the subtle cues and is the first to identify your dream.

Most people have a social network and a professional network. People in your social network should be able to help you maximize your effectiveness, decrease your stress and build your confidence. They should act as a sounding board, tell you you're great and that you can do it and be there to nudge you along. People in your professional network introduce you to others, help you understand the politics in a situation, help you learn skills and mentor you. These two networks are usually different but can become one. As Libby explained, *"I'm a big believer in networking. I do a lot of networking in New York. I had a year of outplacement. I had coaches. I went to a lot of workshops and support groups and I took advantage of every single thing that year that outplacement had to offer in terms of courses and getting to know yourself and getting in touch with what I wanted to do next in my life. I met a lot of fabulous people. I networked like crazy. I met and now have a lot of very close friends. We really supported each other through very lengthy transitions. I wasn't alone in the process. I learned so much from my professional networking groups."*

Beware of the dark side of relationships—those relationships that are competitive and destructive. These people may mask themselves as supporters but are deadly, and may pose a huge obstacle for getting on with dreaming. Josie: *"I'm part of many women's financial groups. And I found some of them to be supportive, some not. I've found some of them are deathly competitive and most women my age, middle or late fifties, are in transition. They are looking for work. Some are supportive and some are just lethal. It's one-on-one. I've learned who to go to and who to stay away from when I need help."*

If you find yourself in an unsatisfactory or draining relationship or if the stress of it preoccupies your thoughts, beware—it can sap your energy and prevent you from achieving your dream. This is an indicator that you need to take action.

Reflect on the following questions about your relationships. This will prepare you for the Resource Checkup.

- Who are the important people in my life?
- Why are these people important? What can I count on them for (to make me feel good, to give me encouragement, to be my sounding board, to help)?
- Who are the people in my professional network?
- How would I call upon them to help?
- Do I have relationships that cause me stress or pain?
- Do I need other people to help me realize my dream?

---

## Exercise: The Resource Checkup
(Time to complete: 10 minutes)

You need to ask yourself: "Do I have the resources to achieve my dreams?" To answer this question, you must take stock and assess those areas that are working and those that need attention. When you take stock, you are surveying what resources you have, as well as their quality. You might say, "I have lots of friends and they are there whenever I need them." Or you might say, "I know lots of people but I can't count on many of them to help me."

You begin with what you have and build from there. You might enjoy reasonable health but you may need to exercise more. You might have a good job but need to supplement your income. You might enjoy your husband and friends but be concerned about your frail mother. The questions you answered throughout this chapter should have given you some ideas about problem areas. Now is the time to gather your thoughts about each of the three resources.

The Resource Checkup allows you to make an inventory of what resources you have, so you can decide what needs attention and then set realistic goals. You can do your own simple checkup by following the example below. Remember, this is only an example and you need to conduct your own checkup.

## EXAMPLE: RESOURCE CHECKUP

|  | Working Well | Needs Attention |
|---|---|---|
| Health | • Feeling energetic and in good health<br>• Minor problems under control with medication<br>• Well-balanced diet | • Exercise<br>• Sleep<br>• Stress reduction |
| Finance | • On budget<br>• Spending in control<br>• Some retirement savings | • Rainy-day savings<br>• Long-term savings |
| Relationships | • Getting along with partner<br>• Great friends | • Worry about one child<br>• Worry about and caring for ill mother |

Now complete your own resource checkup. As you can see, this is your personal checkup, your own view, not somebody else's view of you. You are more likely to devote the attention, time and energy to making it work if *you* do the evaluation rather than accepting someone else's. We don't know of anyone who successfully quit smoking without deciding to do it themselves.

---

Once you have a realistic assessment of each resource, you need to decide where you want to direct your energies. It is difficult to try to work on everything at the same time.

> **Tip: Focus on what is most important to you and where you are most likely to meet with success. Gather more information—read books, visit websites (see opposite page). Find a counselor, a coach or a good friend to help you. Get the help you need.**

Now that you have an inventory of your strengths and the resources needed to realize your dream, you still need to be aware of some myths or obstacles that may get in your way. You then will have the relevant material and information to create your road map.

## Resources

### Websites:

- The John D. and Catherine T. MacArthur Foundation Research Network on Successful Midlife Development http://midmac.med.harvard.edu
- The National Center on Women and Aging for the POWER Center http://heller.brandeis.edu/bestresources
- Canadian Women's Health Network http://www.hc-sc.gc.ca/english/women/cewh.htm
- MidLifeMentor.com™ http://midlifementor.com

### Books:

- *Who Moved My Cheese? An Amazing Way to Deal with Change in Your Work and in Your Life* by Spencer Johnson, Kenneth H. Blanchard (Foreword) (New York: Putnam Pub Group [Paper], September 1, 1998).
- *The Wealthy Barber: Eveyone's Commonsense Guide to Becoming Financially Independent*, 3rd ed. by David Chilton (Roseville, CA: Prima Publishing, December 1, 1997).
- *Smart Women Finish Rich: 9 Steps to Achieving Financial Security and Finding Your Dreams.* Updated and revised 2nd ed. by David Bach (New York: Broadway Books, January 8, 2002)
- *Handbook for Midlife Development* by Lachman, Margie E., ed. (New York: John Wiley & Sons, 2001).

seven

# MYTHS: THE HIJACKERS OF DREAMS

*MONETTE: "WHEN I LOST MY JOB, I was forty-six years old. I remember going to a labor lawyer to negotiate a severance package. He basically hit me so hard by saying, 'At forty-six, as far as the job market is concerned, you're out. Don't look at the jobs you had in your thirties and forties—whether you're good at it or not—because at your age they are not even going to look at you.' At the time I lost my job, this statement was perceived as reality, not myth. So if it is not a myth and indeed a fact, then you have to turn it around. I looked around and said, 'I'm going to take this as an opportunity' rather than as 'Oh my God, what am I going to do now?' Losing my job ended up being positive. Over the last ten years the perception that you cannot get a job after forty-five has been changing. People have lost their jobs and are going back to work in their sixties."*

While ageism is certainly pervasive in the workplace, the premise for ageism is based on myths. These myths are about people's physical and mental abilities at a particular age and they say that you are no longer suited to traditional work. These myths or conventional wisdoms are not based in reality.

Monette's experience highlights that myths about age can restrict your dreams; that is, if you buy into them. The next time somebody tells you a joke about "not being able to teach an old dog new tricks" or informs you that you are "over the hill," instead of chuckling, you might want to think about what is being conveyed and their insidious negativism. It is bad enough that these myths get perpetuated but even worse that many women believe them to be true. In believing them to be true you may have unwittingly erected invisible barriers that serve to hijack your dreams.

In this chapter you will learn the answers to these questions:

- What is a myth?
- Which four prevailing myths about the Vantage Years hijack dreams and how can you debunk these myths?

## What Is a Myth?

According to the *Oxford Dictionary*, a myth is widely held, may be taken as truth but is a false notion embodying popular ideas on natural or social phenomena. Common myths with which boomers grew up are: "Father knows best," "Marriage is forever," "A woman's place is in the kitchen," "If you haven't done it by now you will never do it" and so on. There are a number of prevailing myths about women in midlife which many of you believe. You may believe that *all* women experience empty-nest syndrome when their children leave home; that you are the sandwich generation taking care of young children and aging parents simultaneously; and that everyone has a midlife crisis. Several scientific studies have found little evidence to support these myths. While some of these conditions are experienced by some women, for most they do not reach the crisis stage.[1, 2]

One of the biggest myths older boomers believed was that a woman did not need an education and that her husband would take care of her. For so many of you this did not turn out to be true. Another myth that you may still buy into is that having a man in your life will guarantee your happiness. Most of you now know that in order to be fulfilled, you need more than just a man (even if he is great). You need your own identity.

Sibylle told us what happened to her after her marriage of thirty-two years dissolved: *"I think it took me a lot longer than most to grow up. I was married and I believed the fairy tale. I never thought about having to go out to work and to support myself. I never worried about those things. Obviously I should have."*

As Nicole said: *"One myth is that a woman doesn't need an education. She's going to be taken care of by her husband. I left home at twenty to marry because that was the only way to leave home, which I wanted to do very badly. All I had at that point was a high-school education plus secretarial school. So I went to work. That marriage lasted four years. I threw everything out at the same time: religion, family, marriage, and said, 'No, that is not what I want.' The second myth that I had bought into, and that I had to deal with, was that the man is going to make you happy. It didn't work the first time. It worked the second time because we were very much in love. However, it didn't answer all the questions. I ended up in a situation where I was a widow at thirty with a young child. At that time there didn't seem to be careers for women. So I went back to school. Yes, education was open to me all of a sudden."*

We often rely on myths to tell us how to act in situations that are uncharted or where the norms of behavior are ill defined. Vantage Women are stepping into those waters when they retire from work or when their children leave home. For the boomers who are facing this situation in large numbers, the waters are uncharted and the rules of behavior have yet to be written. There is a real danger of latching on to prevailing myths and accepting them as truth.

## Which Four Prevailing Myths About the Vantage Years Hijack Dreams?

Today, many of the myths Vantage Women are confronting relate to ageism. Although you may have encountered sexism in the workplace, this may be the first time you are also confronting ageism. Ageism exists in the workplace. It is even more daunting than the glass ceiling ever was. Sexism and ageism are a deadly combination. The ageism myth serves to marginalize certain individuals by defining who is in the "in group" and who is in the "out group." Young is in, old is out. This chapter is not about fighting ageism in corporations, although that might be a worthy battle for some. This chapter is about understanding how those myths can erode self-worth and feelings of hope, and how battling them, even in your own mind, can help you achieve your dreams.

There are many myths out there, but we have selected four that can be damaging and hazardous for dreaming:

- Myth 1: You can't teach an old dog new tricks.
- Myth 2: You are over the hill after fifty; the decline begins at forty.
- Myth 3: Retirement means the end of the game.
- Myth 4: One size fits all.

Each society develops ideas about how things work or ought to work. For example, men are better suited to working outside the home; women are better suited to caring for children at home. These ideas are not fixed in stone and can change as a function of your own personal circumstance, what society needs and the prevailing culture's views. Western society's views on women and work changed in the 1940s when men went off to war and there was a shortage of "man" power. Surprisingly, women suddenly became suited to working outside the home and were sent to the factories. This is an example of how society changed its view of women and work driven by circumstance.

In the same way that society constructs ideas about what are appropriate or inappropriate behaviors for its citizens, so too individuals construct their own views of how the world operates and how they should behave. After the Second World War, many reverted to the belief that a woman's place was in the home, but there were many others, women and men, who did not buy into this idea and, in fact, changed the world of work.

Myths can be debunked by examining the assumptions underlying them and the evidence that supports or refutes them. Remember: Myths are sustained on misinformation and half-truths. Myths feed attitudes and attitudes feed behavior. If you are going to change behavior, begin changing attitudes by confronting the myth.

In the 1990s, the Bank of Montreal was a leader in debunking myths about their women employees. Until then, such myths had stopped many women from advancing in their careers. The bank report called *Task Force on the Advancement of Women* was groundbreaking in providing hard data. It was a commonly held view in the bank that women were not being promoted because on average they were younger than men, had less experience and had fewer years of education. In examining the data, Deanna and the task force proved that men and women employees were the same average age, with the same number of years of education and experience. These prevailing myths were simply excuses, accepted as fact, for not promoting women equally. Once the task force had confronted and debunked "cherished" myths, the bank became a recognized leader in the advancement of women and an advocate for diversity and equitable employment opportunities for all, not only for women.

## Myth 1: You can't teach an old dog new tricks

Many people believe that as we age we lose our ability to learn new things. We cite failing memory, aversion to change and inability to learn as evidence to sustain this myth. Why do you believe that you can't teach an old dog new tricks? You may have found that with age, your memory is not as sharp as it was and that it is more difficult to acquire and retain new information. This myth is reinforced in popular culture with jokes and cartoons about forgetful, vulnerable, rigid middle-agers. These jokes and cartoons are taken as reflections of reality. If you believe this myth, you are also buying into the assumption that as you age you become more set in your ways and, therefore, you are more reluctant to try new things.

**The reality:** Research weighs in to say that you are never too old to learn. Scientists have found that learning is life-long, not reserved just for the young. Your brain is wired for continuous learning from cradle until grave unless there is some organic disease or pathology that limits learning. The brain is a beehive of continuous activity. Positron emission tomography (PET) imaging of the brain has revealed that new neural pathways are always being created, strengthened, pruned with every activity. Every day you take in information through your senses, process it, transform it and store it for later retrieval and recall. You cannot help but learn whether or not you intend to, plan for it or are aware that it is happening. It *is* happening. People are wired to understand and to know. Without understanding and knowing, humans would not be able to survive, let alone adapt to and function in environments that are ever-changing.

Learning is also about a "can-do" attitude. How many older people do you know who claimed that they could not learn how to work the Internet, but became knowledgeable about it as soon as they realized how much they were missing by not being plugged in? If it is true that learning never stops, then why do so many believe they cannot learn, citing memory deterioration as the primary culprit? Why do so many forget things and blame it on a "senior's moment"? Each of you can probably remember an incident where a name did not roll off your tongue or you could not place a familiar face or you misplaced a to-do list. So many women in the Vantage Years suddenly become aware of their failing memory, having previously taken a good memory for granted.

Though the speed of processing or retrieving the information may have slowed, the information is not lost. Many of you can recall meeting someone on the street or at a party who looks familiar but you cannot remember their name or where you met them. You will likely remember that person's name thirty minutes later or even the next day. Generally, you do recall things and people that matter. You may find you have to develop strategies to compensate for these "lapses," such as telling people you will get back to them and giving yourself more time to respond.

As infants and children grow there is a rapid increase in capacity to remember in many different areas. This capacity then levels off in the adult and middle years before showing some decline only in the later years (65+) and, even then, in very few areas involving memory. This is hardly surprising when you think that childhood is a time of discovery and setting down the millions of neural pathways. Once these have been created, there are fewer new pathways needed. In fact, depending on what is used, some areas of memory improve, others remain unchanged and very few show decline.

Memory and learning across ages are equal but different. In debunking Myth 1, the question is not whether your memory is as good at this age as it was when you were younger, but more whether you still have the willingness and interest to learn new things. Your memory and the way you learn is different in the Vantage Years from the way you learned when you were a child or a young adult because your needs and requirements are very different. Your understanding of how the world works and your knowledge base is more comprehensive at this age than in your youth. You already know so much. Learning is about much more than just memory. Learning is about knowing and understanding. This is good news for Vantage Women because they have learned to make connections, listen carefully, have confidence in their opinions and be thoughtful. Ultimately it means, when starting a new job, we must learn less than a younger person would.

In your youth, you learned information to get ahead or to get a job. Many Vantage Women are finding that they now enjoy learning simply for the sake of learning. Pat returned to university for a first degree at the age of fifty. *"I changed more with that degree. You learn how to formulate your ideas, how to express them. I used to have an answer but I couldn't explain it. Education alters your mind."*

Memory is about understanding and knowing how the world operates. Deanna Kuhn, professor of psychology at Columbia University,[3] suggests that how we adapt to new situations is a function of what we know (knowledge), what it means (comprehension), why we know (purpose) and how we manage knowing (meta-strategic control).

The myth that you can't teach an old dog new tricks prevails. Within some workplaces it is even believed that older workers are too difficult to train, do not perform at high enough standards, are paid too much in salary and benefits and are too inflexible. This myth has not been supported. In fact, research points to the contrary. McEvoy and Cascio examined the job performance in more than ninety-six studies of 38,983 workers who were between the ages of seventeen and sixty. They came from a variety of professions—engineers, scientists, managers, nurses and nonprofessional jobs. The study found that there was no difference in job performance between older and younger workers.[4]

Vantage women are at a distinct advantage because they better understand others and themselves, have less to prove and have more confidence to make the right decision faster. Your experience, what you already know and what you can readily infer gives you the edge to adapt to many new situations and to look at things in novel ways.

## Myth 2: You are over the hill after fifty; the decline begins at forty

This myth is based on the observation that midlife is a time of noticeable change in our physical and mental capacities. Up until recently, the decline was thought to start in our forties and, spurred on by menopause, accelerate into our fifties. In the work world, the stereotypical midlife and older woman is portrayed as unattractive, slow and past her prime.

If you believe in this myth you are buying into the idea that development proceeds with gains in the early years followed by losses later on. It is hardly surprising that many believe that older people don't have value.

**The reality:** Your experiences should tell you this is just not true. No matter how grown-up you are, you never stop developing. In fact, throughout the life span, development is characterized by both gains and losses at every age. Infants lose most of their reflexes within the first four to six months of life as they gain in intentional behavior. Infants lose their desire to crawl when they gain in their ability to walk and run.

For adults, the losses after forty vary considerably from person to person. In fact, chronological age is not as good a predictor of developmental changes in later adulthood as it was in childhood. There is great variability in the pace at which people lose function. Just look around you for the evidence. There are some fifty-year-olds using canes because of knee and hip deterioration while others are running marathons.

You may first have become aware of the aging process by the subtle and not-so-subtle changes in your outward appearance and changes in your physical strength and stamina. You may recall the feeling of horror on discovering that first gray hair or the almost imperceptible lines that first appeared around your eyes or mouth. These telltale signs were some of the earliest indicators of loss. You may have tried to erase wrinkles and prop up sagging skin, cover graying hair, whiten teeth, build body mass, strengthen bones in an attempt to reverse or, at the very least, slow down the aging process.

The good news is that loss is gradual and less perceptible to others than to you. What you can do is select goals and life tasks that are most meaningful to optimize the strengths that you have and compensate for those you do not have. It was the life-span psychologists Baltes and Baltes[5] who identified selective optimization with compensation (SOC) as an important process that operates at all stages of development. You may have noticed that you concentrate better first thing in the morning and therefore select to optimize your memory by working at this time. Or you may have noticed that you are working shorter hours and producing at the same or even higher levels because you have learned to work smarter. Or you may have switched to power walking rather than to jogging to compensate for the deterioration in your knee joints. Or you may be choosing to do things that give you the most pleasure, that are the most interesting, that bring the most satisfaction.

Women who are going through their Vantage Years with the most success intuitively preserve and conserve energy and operate at their maximum capacity. They are drawing on their inner strength of self-regulation. They know what they want, they know where to put their efforts to get best results and they know how to work most effectively. If you find yourself regularly exhausted and frustrated, think of ways to prevent this from happening. Recognizing signs of "shutdown," and taking a nap or a break may solve this problem.

With a more positive attitude during the Vantage Years, gains outweigh losses. Your emotional and cognitive capacities can compensate for some of your diminishing physical capacities. You may find that you are more resilient in the face of disappointment and more adaptable to a changing environment. Because you know who you are and are more accepting of yourself, confidence replaces the confusion and self-doubt of youth. This new-found confidence is reflected in a surer you. Jane told us "*I was married for fifteen years, but when that ended I was free to do whatever I wanted. In a way, that was a blessing, although it was devastating at the time. That was years ago. I had my sixtieth birthday last week and I am good until I am seventy, either doing what I am doing or something else. And after that who knows?"*

How you feel about yourself at this age is very much related to your attitude—how you frame things. You can choose to focus on the losses or on the gains. It's up to you. If you believe in this myth—that you are over the hill after fifty—you will be stymied in creating your dream.

## Myth 3: Retirement means the end of the game

Retirement has traditionally been the time after a person stopped working. All paid work ceased once you were given the gold watch. You were expected to go away, withdraw from society and from the workplace, retreat from public view into a more sheltered and secluded environment. You traded a job for bridge, golf and baby-sitting grand-children. The dictionary defines retirement as a perma-nent withdrawal from normal service. It is no coincidence that when they "retire" a ship, it goes straight to the scrap yard. As Kate expressed, *"I am in my late fifties and would like to think of the ages between sixty and eighty as active and healthy. However, there is a stereotype in society of what happens then. That period is definitely considered 'rocking chair country.'"* If you have bought into this myth, then you believe that anything you haven't done by now, you will never do.

You might also believe that women worry less than men about retirement because they have so many other roles that fill their time: wife, mother, grandmother, friend. Or you may believe that women adjust better to retirement because their identities are not defined by their careers. These too are myths.

**The reality:** Gwen observed: *"Women have more of a capacity to reinvent themselves."* For many, retirement is eagerly anticipated and welcomed as a time to change pace, rhythm and activity in the conduct of one's life. Bernard Lewis, the acclaimed Middle East expert, continues writing well into his eighties. He quotes an unknown source that said, "Retirement is the time to change the tires and go full speed ahead."

For others, however, the word *retirement* fills them with a sense of dread. No wonder. Retirement, particularly unplanned or forced, is a cause of major trauma and depression. Retirement ranks among the top ten most stressful events with which a person has to cope.[6]

Women retiring today at the age of fifty-five may experience this event very differently from women retiring at the age of seventy. For most women retiring at age fifty-five, their identities were very much defined by their work and professional status. As Nan Bauer-Maglin and Alice Radosh wrote in their book *Women Confronting Retirement: A Nontraditional Guide,* "Never has there been as extensive a population of women who faced retirement so unsure of their worth without their jobs." They go on to explain that when identity is tied up with work, it is harder to slam that door closed. This period is particularly difficult for this generation of women who find their work meaningful, rewarding, socially relevant and enjoyable.[7]

To succeed in retirement, is not to retire from something but to graduate to something else or to move from one dream to a new dream. Impending retirement is a good turning point at which to reappraise your life and revisit your dreams. Remember, retirement is something that happens to you; a reappraisal is something that you do for yourself. Researchers have found that older people who are invested in long-term goals, even those individuals well into their seventies and eighties, are psychologically healthier than those who have disengaged and retired from life.[8] As Eleanor Roosevelt remarked: "The future belongs to those who believe in the beauty of their dreams."

Michal found herself reappraising her life and career after her husband retired from being a temple cantor. *"I had been working as a lawyer for the army and we were given notice that the base was closing and would be moved to a new location. It wasn't very easy for a woman at my age trying to break either out of the public sector into the private sector or to even get another job in St. Louis, where we were living. One of the jobs that I applied for was as an administrative law judge. However, it was in New York City, which meant we would have to move. My husband was retired and after his being the primary wage earner all these years, now I was the primary wage earner. I grew up believing that you go where your husband is . . . I didn't even consider that he would move for my job. But he did."*

The reason you are not at the end of the game is that the game is ever expanding. Look around you. Oprah Winfrey, who guides and inspires others to make the most of their talents, and Bette Midler, the entertainer par excellence, are but a couple of famous women who continue to pursue their dreams well into their fifties and sixties. Madeleine Albright, the former secretary of state in the Clinton administration, wrote in her memoir *Madam Secretary:* "I was taught to strive not because there were any guarantees of success but because the act of striving is in itself the only way to keep faith with life."[9]

Many women want to remain at work because they want to stay productive, earn money, have social contacts and make a contribution. When they retire, they still have these same needs. What women appreciate at this age is that making a contribution can be done in many different ways, not only in a formal work environment: volunteerism, philanthropy, continuous learning.

Over fifty years ago, Erik Erikson, the well-known psychoanalyst and life-span developmental psychologist, identified the task of the middle-adult years as a choice between generativity or stagnation. Generativity means leaving something behind that is beyond your own life. It is about mentoring the younger generation and leaving a legacy. Research has borne this out. Those who are engaged in generative activities such as parenting, teaching, mentoring, guiding, inspiring, coaching and leading report greater feelings of well-being and higher life satisfaction.[10, 11] Anna told us how she mentors others and wishes she had had the type of mentoring she now provides: *"What I am doing now is mentoring a young woman. I have been talking to her about her life and what she is going to do. She is always asking my advice and I guess you can say she is my protegé. If someone had pushed me earlier, I would have started my business in my twenties but I got caught up in other agendas."*

Companies are retiring people earlier as a way of containing costs. The focus has been on older workers because their salaries and benefits are more costly. However, the winds of change are beginning to shift direction. Companies are starting to recognize that they need the knowledge and skills of older, more experienced workers and are recalling them. In fact, we saw this happen in the health-care system that went from a nursing surplus, where many nurses were given lucrative buyout packages, to a severe nursing shortage, with a serious lack of experienced nurses. This was prevalent from the late 1990s throughout North America. Experienced nurses found themselves at a premium, with administrators begging them to reenter the workforce.

In fact, companies are just beginning to reflect the new societal reality that has been written into law. The Age Discrimination in Employment Act was amended in 1986, banning mandatory retirement.[12]

Retirement is not the end of the game. Twenty-five percent of people over sixty years of age continue to work, at least part-time. In fact, many of us are seeing our parents work well into their seventies and eighties. In her mid-sixties, Deanna's mother, Lottie, went back to work after forty years out of the labor force. Now in her mid-eighties, she continues to take the subway to her part-time job as a bookkeeper.

The big change is in who will direct your career at this stage of life. For many of you, your career will be directed by you, not your employer. And your career will be tailored by you to reflect your dream. More people are managing their own careers because of the reams of layoffs in the traditional workplace. More and more people are self-employed, becoming their own boss. Germaine Greer's landmark book on menopause, *The Change,* foresaw that women's desire to continue to work would not be in sync with society's need to retire them. She advised these women who were told to mind their own business . . . to get their own business.[13] Sound advice.

## Myth 4: One size fits all

Although used in the retail industry to size women's clothing, "one size fits all" has become a metaphor for other practices in other aspects of life. If you subscribe to this myth, you believe that everyone fits a pattern. Your view is that you have to fit into a mold and follow someone else's plan. You also may believe that there is only one route to a destination, and if you do not take that route, you may not get there. This may explain why you are encountering difficulties making the transition through the Vantage Process and placing obstacles in your path to dreaming.

**The reality:** One size, in fact, fits no one. The idea that one size fits all is a huge myth because it is based on the average and there is no such thing as an average. Think of what makes up the average. It is the sum of everyone's score divided by the number of scores used. It doesn't represent an individual. It blurs unique differences.

Researchers are discovering that no two individuals in this world have the same DNA, live in the same environment or enjoy the same tastes in food, drink, clothes or color. That's why there are thousands of diet and exercise books, thousands of books on health, finances and relationships, and you have not seen the last of them. No one has discovered the magic bullet because there is no single magic bullet. There are as many ways of living as there are people.

The growing acknowledgment of the uniqueness of each person is reflected in the growing trend of customization. Those industries that have acknowledged that uniqueness has to be respected in their product or service have done exceedingly well. Computer companies understood this need. An example is Dell Inc. whose business model is popular not only because of the price and quality of its product, but because you can go to the internet and customize a computer to your needs. Think of Starbucks where you can mix and match any of the components they offer—coffees, teas, milk, foams, flavorings—to suit your specific taste. Think of the car industry where the basic car is tailored to reflect your personal preferences based on the packages and options you select. Banks customize investment portfolios based on the customer's unique level of risk.

People begin with the generic and then need to find the formula that best suits them. It's the continuous search for the best fit between what's out there and your own body type, personality, lifestyle and self-discipline. Goodness-of-fit is discussed in Chapter 5—Strengths. The future trend is for pharmaceuticals to tailor dose and drug composition to match your unique biological makeup. And this trend of customization for the "customer of one" will permeate all aspects of your life.

Understanding what makes you unique is a good thing. In fact, it is your uniqueness that can enable you to achieve your dream, because your dream is specific to you. This is your driver of success. The challenge is finding the right match or creating the right match. Bill Gates, of Microsoft, did not fit into the round holes and expectations of his industry, so he responded by creating square holes and a new business model in which to fit. He created his own fit.

Don't allow the myths that hijack dreams to hijack *your* dreams. You must build your own dreams that are a reflection of you and a reflection of you in today's work environment. This table summarizes the myths and realities.

## MYTHS AND REALITIES

| Myth | Reality |
|---|---|
| You can't teach an old dog new tricks. | You are never too old to learn. |
| You are over the hill after fifty; the decline begins at forty. | The best is yet to come. Life is a series of peaks and valleys, gains and losses. |
| Retirement means the end of the game. | Retire and full speed ahead. Freedom fifty-five, sixty-five, seventy-five and beyond. |
| One size fits all. | One size fits no one. |

In the next chapter, you will determine how ready you are to write your personal road map for achieving your dreams.

eight

# READINESS: IF NOT NOW, WHEN?

MICHELLE, AN EDUCATOR SAID, *"I was at a turning point around thirty-five. I was sitting in this school and I was so full of ideas. I had just come back from a conference that had been wonderful. I had projects that I wanted to do and students who had just won a competition. I looked around for somebody I could talk to. And there was no one. So I decided I needed to change. Another school approached me to run a media program. I jumped at the opportunity because I was ready. I knew I couldn't stay where I was. I had this feeling that, ugh! I was lonely and I felt stuck. And I realized that something had to change. I think I had to get to the point where I felt caught in the corner. I knew change had to happen but I didn't know what form it was going to take. And it has taken so many forms."*

In her mid-sixties, Gretta found her public life taking a new direction. She recounts the story of how she was told that she had been named the first woman chancellor of

McGill University. *"I was moving houses and was in the midst of packing when the chairman of the board of governors called to say he wanted to come over. I was on two or three university committees and there was a new chairman. I'd been working late the night before and I had told the secretary general and chairman: 'I'm not going to be coming in tomorrow. I've got to pack. I've just got to pack.'*

*"I was packing. I was in blue jeans and running shoes. When the chairman called me, he sounded worried. He asked, 'What are you doing?' And I said, 'I told you, I'm packing. I don't want to see you. I don't want to see anybody.' He said, 'Oh, I've got to come over, just for a minute. It won't take me long. I promise you.'*

*"I had been rude, so I thought I had better make him a cup of coffee. It was nine in the morning and I put two cups of coffee in the machine and the doorbell rang. I opened the front door and in came a delegation in their best clothes and there were five of them. The chairman comes in and behind him are the principal and all these other people.*

*"I'm completely unprepared—my hair uncombed. He says, 'Good morning, Madam Chancellor.'*

*"Now I thought I was going to faint. I really thought, this cannot be happening to me. I said, 'But I've only made two cups of coffee.' So he said, 'What do you think about this?' I said, 'I'm not thinking about it at all. I can't possibly . . . I can't possibly be a chancellor.' And the chairman answered, 'Why not?' And I said, 'There is nothing I hate worse in the world than speaking in public.' And he said, 'Speaking in public? You won't have to speak much in public. I suppose you'd have to say a little something at convocation but you can say exactly the same thing at every convocation.' I thought of every reason*

*in the world to say no. I was too busy—I had to move. And I didn't know what to do and I actually called my husband. And my husband started to laugh. And he said, 'Well, I'll tell you. It will quicken things up. Recognize right now that you're actually going to do it. But you know, calm yourself because it just wastes a lot of time dithering and you know perfectly well that you are going to do it in the end.'"*

Two women of different ages, in different circumstances, yet both were ready for change. Michelle heeded the early warning signals (Phase 1 of the Vantage Process) and was ready to move on when the opportunity presented itself. On the surface, Gretta had not anticipated this new direction in her life and seemed unready for it. However, her lifetime of experiences had prepared her well for this challenge. She was indeed ready.

In this chapter you will learn the answers to these questions:

- What is readiness?
- Why is readiness a precursor for action?
- How do I get ready?
- How do I fare on the Readiness Assessment Exercise?
- What are the conditions that promote readiness?
- What are the obstacles that affect readiness?
- What are the strategies for getting ready to make change?

## What Is Readiness?

Ready is defined as ". . . completely prepared for action, inclined or disposed, immediately available at the moment."[1] In this chapter, we are talking about being ready to move from one phase of the Vantage Process to the next. We are also talking about being ready to convert your dream into reality—from talking about the dream to creating the dream to living the dream.

You may have found yourself stalled in one phase of the Vantage Process. The only way to move forward is to ready yourself for action or at least be inclined to do so. Taking action is the best way we know to get unstuck and move forward. Remember, the phases in the Vantage Process are not linear; therefore, you can be involved with tasks of more than one phase simultaneously. You can be mourning the loss (Phase 2—Saying Goodbye) while beginning to make plans (Phase 3—Betwixt and Between).

## Why Is Readiness a Precursor for Action?

"Ready, set, go"; "Ready, willing and able"—two familiar sayings about change, and *ready* is the first and key word in both sayings. You have to be ready to even begin to dream. Without readiness there is no change. You may experience the early warning signs of oncoming change, but if you are not open and ready to act, you will ignore or discount them. In fact, you may do everything in your power to resist change, to maintain the status quo.

If you are not open to change, you will be deaf to the signals even if they are loud and clear. You say, "But I was laid off. I was not ready for that." There may have been some signs, even if subtle and unsubstantiated—merger talk, office gossip, your boss leaving, poor annual results.

Even if you missed the early signs and change happened *to* you, it's not too late to ready yourself for the next change: the one dictated by you. Regardless of whether the cues are subtle or obvious, you need to decide when and how you are going to act.

The Vantage Process requires that you prepare. You prepare yourself by building your strengths (Chapter 5), resources (Chapter 6) and dealing with myths (Chapter 7)—just as you ready yourself for a trip by planning the trip, making reservations and packing.

## How Do You Get Ready?

To be ready for change, there are three required elements:[2]

- Triggers
- Desire for change and the intent to take action
- Costs and benefits

These three elements need to be present when you are getting yourself ready to change. There are two exercises in this chapter. The first exercise—Assess Your Readiness—helps you to determine how ready you are for change. The second exercise—The Decisional Balance Sheet—helps you weigh the costs and benefits to improve your readiness.

**Triggers.** Triggers are those events that signal a need for change or action. From our interviews with women, we heard about those signals that triggered them to take action. If you find yourself saying one or more of the following statements, take heed:

- I am feeling restless.
- I am burnt-out and tired.
- I am bored and what once was a challenge is no more.
- I want to feel productive and valued.
- My children are grown and I feel an emptiness.
- We are being transferred to a new city.
- My close friends are ill or dying.
- I need to find an outlet to channel all my energy.
- I was fired.
- My in-basket is no longer a source of surprise.
- I think that retirement will be a form of escape.

**Desire for change and intent to take action.** Recognizing the signals is not enough and feeling the need to change is not enough. You must have a desire for change—motivation—as well as the intent to take action.

Gwen tells her story: *"By forty-five, I had a really exciting and great career. I had great clients, great files, but they didn't turn me on anymore. There just weren't any better files than the ones I was getting. I was doing these things on automatic pilot. But I still had to work those sixty to seventy hours a week. If I had been able to do it in forty hours a week and have a lot of free time, maybe I would have looked at it differently. But I still had to be a slave to my clients. So it was minus, minus. I went to one of those places where they had me do tests on my abilities. And I learned a couple of things about myself that I hadn't figured out, which were useful.*

*I had a client that drove me nuts. He drove me absolutely up the wall. He would never leave me alone. And I remember about a month before I took the decision to leave, I had an unbelievable migraine. I couldn't get up. He tried to reach me and wouldn't let go. And finally my partner had to tell him, 'She's just not well enough to speak to you.' And I think that's what did it for me. 'This guy thinks he owns me. And I will just not let him do this to me . . .' That was the catalyst. That did it for me. I left my position soon after."* Gwen had the desire and intent, and the trigger sparked her to act.

If you have only the desire and not the intention to take action, you inevitably will feel frustrated, angry with yourself and may become depressed. If one of your small dreams is to fit into a size 8 dress, you may have the desire, but without the intent to lose weight you won't go on that diet. You need to make the decision to take action and then to follow through for something to happen.

Some women express a desire for change and they also intend to take action, but they don't know what action to take because they have no clear direction. They have not as yet identified their dreams. That is why finding your dream is critical.

---

## Exercise: Assess Your Readiness
(Time to complete: 10 minutes)

To assess your own readiness for change you may want to complete the readiness assessment exercise on the next page. In this exercise you should place yourself in one of the quadrants in the chart.

**ASSESS YOUR READINESS**

high

Intent to take action

| 3 Work on desire and motivation | 4 Ready |
|---|---|
| 1 Not ready | 2 Work on intent |

low        Desire for change        high

**Key**

**Quadrant 1: Not Ready**
I like the way things are (low desire). I have done nothing and have no intention of doing anything (low intent to take action).

**Quadrant 2: Somewhat ready—need to work on intent**
I feel highly motivated to live my dream and want to change now (high desire) but I have not done anything (low intent to take action).

**Quadrant 3: Somewhat ready—need to work on desire and motivation**
I have investigated and gathered information (high intent to take action) but can't get myself going (low desire).

**Quadrant 4: Ready for change**
I feel highly motivated to live my dream (high desire) and I also have taken steps (high intent). I am ready and set to go.

In this chart the *desire for change* lies along the horizontal axis and the *intent to take action* along the vertical axis, moving from low to high on both axes. You will determine to what degree you have a desire to change on a continuum from low desire to high desire and your intent to actually act, measured from low intent to high intent. Use the key to place yourself in the quadrant that best describes how you feel now.

Your goal is to move into the upper right quadrant where you will have a high desire for change and a high intent to take action. It is only in this quadrant that you are ready for change.

---

**Weighing the costs and benefits.** The third element of readiness involves weighing the costs and benefits of the status quo versus change. The primary way to increase desire and intent is through weighing the costs and benefits of the current situation compared to the uncertain future. People do not move from a known situation to another known situation. You go from a known to an unknown situation, passing through the hallways of uncertainty.

For change to occur, the cost of the status quo must be much higher than the benefits of the status quo, and the benefits of the change must outweigh the costs of the change. Costs include not only financial considerations and the impact they have on other people in your life. Costs also include assaults to your ego, frustration, dissatisfaction and discontent. Sharon wisely observed that *"Although husbands are often your major support, they care so much about you that they may not encourage you to take a big risk at a time when you might need to take such a risk."*

The dream is the new choice. It is only when the benefits of the new dream outweigh the costs of not doing it that you will choose the new dream. When the new dream's benefits outweigh the costs of remaining in the same situation,

184 | dreams have no expiry date

you will be ready to create the plan for turning your dream into reality.

---

## Exercise: Cost/Benefit Assessment

(Time to complete: 30–60 minutes)

You should create a cost/benefit table like the one below to evaluate the benefits and costs associated with your own dream.[3]

### EXAMPLE: COST/BENEFIT ASSESSMENT

| Stay at this Job | | Find my Dream Job | |
| Benefits | Costs | Benefits | Costs |
| --- | --- | --- | --- |
| I know what I'm doing | No fun anymore | Find something that expresses my true self | Compete with younger candidates |
| I get a regular paycheck | I am stressed out | Learn something new; master new skills | May not find a better job than what I have |
| I do well | I feel undervalued | Meet new people | Too busy to look |
| | I am not using my full talents | See new opportunities | May be out of work with no money |

The process of becoming ready for change requires that you compare the costs of the status quo to the costs of the change. The costs of making a change, with new fears and anxieties, may be high. The costs of not changing can be even higher. You have to try to assign a value to both. In his book *The Complete Idiot's Guide to Change Management*, Jeff Davidson summarized this very sentiment: "Moving forward is only possible when the pain of the present state exceeds the cost of the transition state."[4]

You can convince yourself to stay with the status quo by saying to yourself "the devil you know is better than the devil you don't know" or "from the frying pan into the fire." If you are using such arguments to convince yourself to act, it may be that the dream is not clear enough, so that you can't see the benefits. The tipping point in favor of change is to brighten the benefit picture by creating an authentic dream.

Without a dream and a clear picture of the benefits that will accrue, the costs of changing will outweigh the benefits of the change and you will remain in a situation despite the warning signals that it is time to move on. You may then find that change will be thrust upon you by outside forces. It is always valuable to estimate the benefits of your dream and its potential. It is only then that you will be ready to take charge and move on. The only way to take charge—IS—to take charge.

## What Are the Conditions that Promote Readiness?

How can you make yourself ready?

To become ready for change you need to call upon a number of your different strengths. Different types of change require different combinations of strengths and resources. However, every change requires some measure of the following strengths, which we term the six Cs: Courage, Confidence, Curiosity, Chutzpah, Commitment and Control. But remember that all the while, the Clock is ticking.

**Courage.** With just a little courage you will be less inclined to resist change and more inclined to take action, take charge and move in the direction of your dreams. Heidi tells us of her dream to spend time in Paris. *"I had plans this April to go to Paris. I love Paris. I thought I would go but I would have to go alone. I wondered how I would feel and what the experience would be like. I thought, 'I just can't do it.' I did not have the courage. I needed a lot more courage than I had in order to spend time in Paris when I felt alone."*

**Confidence.** Confidence is about how you see yourself and the degree to which you have faith and trust in your own abilities and judgment. You are more likely to be open to new adventure, to see the disadvantages in maintaining the status quo, if you feel that you can bring about change that improves your life. Confidence is associated with a more optimistic attitude. Even if you start off not feeling confident—perhaps someone or something has undermined your confidence—start off doing something that you know you can do. Do things that will build you up, and your confidence will grow. Confidence can be loud or boisterous or can be quiet. Joy described how she rose from volunteer to director of a major university hospital: *"I really acquired my education on a piecemeal basis. I became extremely involved as a volunteer on various boards, and I was quite happy with* *it until my children started university. And then I said, 'I'm not going to play bridge, I'm not going to tea parties. I am going to complete my degree.' The next turning point in my life was when I decided to get a job. I saw an ad in the career section of the newspaper. It didn't say exactly what the job was but it sounded very interesting. It was in the faculty of medicine in the dean's office. And for whatever reason, I got the job. I worked with the dean and students and I loved every minute of it. Some years later I was at a dinner and the director of a teaching hospital asked me to work with him. And I said. 'What at?' 'Oh, we'll figure that out.' So I decided if I don't accept this, I'll never know what I missed. I became director of administrative services, then associate director, until being appointed the director general."*

**Curiosity.** Curiosity and interest are major drivers of change because curious people need to explore the unfamiliar, waters that are uncharted. Curiosity provides that element of surprise that makes life exciting. Curiosity allows you to experiment or try out new things, and that often precedes actually making a permanent change. Curiosity is testing the waters, which readies you for the real thing, as Blema's story illustrates.

Blema, professor emeritus, tells us of changing careers when her curiosity was piqued. *"My children were growing up and I had been teaching political science for twenty years. It was just about the time that I was thinking about what I would do next. I thought, 'Do I really want to teach another two courses? Not really.' My work had been increasing in the field of decision-making. There was more and more literature both in cognitive psychology and also in psychodynamics. I had a very good friend who was an analyst and she said, 'You're so interested. Why don't you become an analyst?' I said, 'What are you talking about? That is ridiculous.' She said, 'No, no, no, it's not. You'll find it fascinating.' So in my fifties, I trained as a psychoanalyst."*

**Chutzpah.** Chutzpah is a Yiddish expression that has found its way into the English lexicon to describe the extra spark it takes, the bit of impudence needed to get yourself where you want to go. You have to have some chutzpah, some nerve, to make change.

Susan recounts the first day on a new job in a different city. *"I remember I phoned my husband the night before my first day on the job as CEO of a provincial economic development corporation. I asked him, 'What does a CEO do?' 'People will bring you problems,' he said, 'and you will solve them.' I had never worked in this city. I had never been the boss. I had never run a development agency. What do I do?"* She did it.

**Commitment.** Commitment is a pledge or an undertaking to something or someone. Commitment involves obligation to yourself and to others. In exchange for making a commitment to deliver, you may have to give up some freedom. Remember Linda of the sweater-design business who told us that she was hesitant to pursue her dreams because of a fear of commitment: *"I was afraid of committing myself to some kind of job or work because I was afraid I couldn't follow through, I couldn't do it well or I couldn't complete it . . . The turning point came for me when I realized I had made a commitment. When you take an order from a customer and someone gives you a deposit, you have to follow through."*

**Control.** When you believe that you have power to be in charge and to bring about change, chances are you will succeed. It is those individuals who are in control and who rely on themselves (see Chapter 5 for a discussion of self-efficacy) who are the most ready and likely to get things done.

Sylvia told us something that happened to her during her college days in the 1950s before she studied medicine and became a doctor. *"At Laurel school they gave a course in car mechanics because the headmistress would not accept having any of her graduates looking stupid at the side of the road. It was wonderful. The following summer, when I was at college, I worked in the Kentucky hills and I was the only one who could drive. There was a state fair that started on Monday and I had to drive a group from the local church on Sunday in their old station wagon. We had three flat tires on the way down and the group got out and went under the trees in the rain and prayed for forgiveness while I changed the tires."* We think they were actually thanking the Lord for sending Sylvia who had the confidence and skills to take control.

**The Clock is ticking.** With age you become more acutely aware of the passage of time and of your own mortality. If you are to realize a dream, you have to capture the moment. Some of the women we interviewed told us that time was a major consideration in deciding to have a baby at forty or to plant that vineyard so that they would be around to reap the joys. For them it was "now or never."

When opportunity presents itself, you have to be prepared to respond. Anne G. told us of her process of getting ready. *"I thought about having a baby on my own for some time. But I thought, 'What would my parents think if I, at the age of forty, had a baby?' Finally, my mother, bless her heart, said, 'Oh by the way, you can always get married at any time but maybe you should have a baby.' A girl should obey her mother. She repeated it a year later in case I hadn't heard."* Some months later, at age forty-one, Anne G. became a single mother of a son, fulfilling her dream.

## What Are the Obstacles that Affect Readiness?

There may be obstacles that impede you from moving forward. These may be emotional issues such as uncontrollable anxiety, low self-esteem, perfectionism, indecisiveness, passivity. You may need to seek professional or other help to overcome these obstacles to readiness.

But these are not the only obstacles to readiness. Like the fears that prevent dreaming (see page 50) there are fears that prevent readiness for change. The biggest fear is the fear of the unknown—uncertainty. Uncertainty is the single largest obstacle to readying yourself for action. Everyone feels uncomfortable with the unknown but some tolerate it better than others. For some uncertainty can become debilitating.

You may find that you are

- uncertain about whether you want to leave the safety and security of life as you know it.
- uncertain that you will be able to succeed or realize your dream.
- uncertain about which is the "right" path to take.
- uncertain about whether you have enough money.

- uncertain that the change will yield greater benefits than the status quo.
- uncertain about how the change will affect your family and lifestyle.

We all know that the best way to overcome fears and uncertainty and the accompanying change is first to face them and then to resolve them.

## What Are the Strategies for Getting Ready to Make Change?

Two ways to make yourself ready are

- improving the benefit side of the cost/benefit assessment.
- creating a financial, social and emotional safety net.

**Improving the benefit side of your cost/benefit assessment.** You should try brainstorming what the benefits of change might be and find ways to put greater weight on the benefits from your Cost/Benefit Assessment, on page 184.

Susan, our CEO with Chutzpa, relates how she weighed the costs and benefits in readying herself for a major life change from working to not working full-time. *"I had the opportunity for a job that required a lot of travel. The job required three to five years to do it properly. The first eighteen months were going to involve a lot of travel across the country. It was an organization that I had a tremendous amount of respect for. Talk about something that crystalized what I wanted to do. My husband and I were sitting at our house when this came up eleven years into our marriage. He just looked at me and I thought, 'So I do this and it's five years from now and great— what if one of us drops dead and I've lost the opportunity to be with my husband for the next five years?' That's really strong for me. I was not prepared to live with my husband just on weekends. Usually my reaction when I get offered things is, 'They want me.' This time, I just said no."*

When Susan really examined the benefits of each decision, she prioritized her values and carefully weighed them. She tipped the scale of benefits in favor of spending the next five years with her husband.

**Creating a financial, social and emotional safety net.** We suggested this strategy of creating a safety net to help you Say Goodbye in Phase 2 of the Vantage Process. Creating a safety net is also a sure-fire way to ready yourself for achieving your dream. If you create a safety net, you have a cushion to absorb some of the risks. When you have something to cushion the risk, you will be able consider options that you might otherwise be too afraid to entertain. A safety net also considerably widens the possibilities for your dreams.

Safety nets can be financial, social, emotional. Even if you do not plan to take a leap of faith, such as leaving a job before you have secured something else, building a safety net is wise. It allows you to be ready for all eventualities and opportunities.

When you are getting ready to work on the plans for your dream, it helps to communicate to others that this change will be of benefit not only to you but to them as well, and at the very least, it won't affect them negatively. It is important to get your support team onside when contemplating change, because the support of family, friends and colleagues is an essential resource that you will call upon to make your dream happen.

One way to do this is to convince the naysayers of the positive aspects. The point here is to sell the idea of your change to everyone—not to win but to win them over. But remember, you can't wait for others to give you the permission to realize your dreams. The power is not another person's to give. You have to create your own readiness if you are to bring about change in your life, even in the face of some skepticism or negativity from others.

Hélène recounted her plan to return to studies in her late forties. *"I'm going to go back and do the doctorate. I remember the first time I thought about it and my husband said to me, 'What do you need this for? You have everything you need. You're going to lose money doing this. What for?' And I said, 'I'm not getting enough out of my teaching. Life is too easy. I need to do this.' I did it for me."* Sometimes partners are the biggest challenge because your change affects their status quo. They may not be interested in changing their current situation and may actively resist. Convincing spouses may take work, but in the end, they can be the best allies.

Consider Alta's state of readiness and her husband's support. Alta, after a long career as a teacher and community worker, realized it was time to retire. She told us how she asked herself and her family, *"Do I have to get sick before I allow myself the privilege of saying I'd like to retire from what I am currently doing? I'd like to take courses. I'd like to do community work on my own. I want to enjoy my family. I want to be able to travel with my husband. My husband traveled a lot on business. I couldn't go. I was always working. So he said, 'Go for it.' So I did."* She was supported by her husband who kept saying to her, *"You know life isn't a dress rehearsal."*

Now that you have assessed your readiness for change, you can proceed to creating your road map.

nine

# ROAD MAP: MAKING IT HAPPEN

*Go confidently in the direction of your dreams.*
*Live the life you've imagined.*
> —HENRY DAVID THOREAU

*Those who say it can't be done are usually*
*interrupted by those who are doing it.*
> —ANONYMOUS

REMEMBER LINDA WHO IS LIVING HER DREAM. *"I gradu-*
*ated in the sixties from university with a B.A. in English and*
*fine arts and was a high-school teacher for three years until I*
*had my first child. I stayed at home taking care of my two*
*children, but after a few years I needed to do something more.*
*My father-in-law owned a travel agency so I went to work for*
*him part-time because my husband and I really loved travel-*
*ing. On the side, I was knitting as a hobby. I was starting to*
*design my own sweaters and knit things for myself and for my*

*children. I wasn't enjoying the travel business, so I decided that I would try to make a business out of knitting. I created a small collection of sweaters, which I had made myself, put them in a bag and started hitting the various terrific boutiques in Montreal. And the very first day out, I got a huge order. I built up a small cottage industry. I designed hand-knitted sweaters and sold them in Canada and in New York. And that went very well. One of my biggest clients, aside from the stores that I sold to, was the then Canadian Prime Minister's wife, Mila Mulroney. This was very lucky for me because she and her husband traveled all over the world and in addition to knitting her sweaters, I also made sweaters for the First Ladies of the countries she visited . . . that was a lot of fun and I really enjoyed doing that. My business came to a natural end when Mila's husband was no longer Prime Minister, the New York store closed and I was tired. And this all happened in the same year. I decided that this is the time for me to do something else. I just ended my business. I closed it down.*

*"And for the next five years I searched for something else to do with my hands, something creative. I tried a bunch of different things. I took some classes in furniture painting. I slugged away at that for a year or so. And I thought, 'maybe I'll make a business out of that.' I decided not to. I didn't really love it. Then, I tried making cushions out of antique fabrics because I had a sewing machine. But I really didn't like doing that either. And I never tried to sell them. I just made a few and threw them around my house and I decided, 'No, it was not going to be that.' I needed something creative that was going to give me a lot of satisfaction and take up most of my time.*

*"I zeroed in on cake decorating. I was in a bookstore one day and saw a book written by a woman famous for her fabulous,*

*imaginative, incredible cakes. So I bought her book and looked through it. The book sat in my kitchen for a year. It totally intimidated me. I didn't think that I could do this. And then one day, I decided to do a cake from her easy section. I tried it. It wasn't so difficult. I realized I could do it. So, basically, from this book I taught myself how to decorate cakes. Then I started making them as gifts so at least people could see what I could do. I tested the market in this way. When I built up enough confidence I said, 'OK, this is a business and I'm going to do this.' And I started selling my cakes. I built up a cake-design business—Edible Art—60 percent wedding cakes and all kinds of milestone cakes . . . I've done television work. I've done magazine work. And it goes on and on."*

Linda's journey may seem somewhat circuitous and not very focused, but in fact, all the while, she had her eyes set on her vision of being creative. She went through all the stages of the Vantage Process of Chapter 4, the catalytic event, saying goodbye, betwixt and between, creating the dream and now she is living the dream. In reading Linda's story you can see that planning the road map of your dream is not a linear process and there may be detours along the way.

Now that you have identified your destination—your dream—analyzed your strengths and resources, debunked the myths about aging and assessed your level of readiness to make your dream happen, you are equipped to create your own road map. This might be a good time to review your dream sheet and the list of values that you created in Chapter 3. Keep both beside you as you proceed through these last chapters. The challenge now is to create a road map that will take you to your destination. The act of creating this road map should be familiar to you—it is the act of planning.

Planning is crucial for success. It helps you to set the course of action, to stay focused on the destination and not to veer off course. It also helps you to resume the course when you have fallen off. Remember, no journey is without its bumps in the road.

Don't fast-forward this process . . . you don't want to miss it all. Both the process and the destination (realizing the dream) are critical. Creating a meaningful plan or road map requires thinking, patience, tenacity and time.

The most successful plans are written down and are detailed. However, if your style is to keep things in your head, a well-thought-out but unwritten plan may work for you. You can even be a planner without being deliberate about or aware of the planning process. There is a continuum between planning and not-planning and you can place yourself anywhere along it.

Those of you who "go with the flow," who resist formalizing a plan of action or who are not as comfortable with plans for fear of sacrificing spontaneity and creativity may be surprised to find this chapter helpful. We, too, value spontaneity. We encourage creativity. Planning and spontaneity are not mutually exclusive. Quite the opposite. Good planning allows you to take advantage of unexpected opportunities. Good planning promotes creativity and makes you more receptive to new ideas.

An effective way to achieve your dreams is to think of taking a journey to a destination. In planning a journey to a destination, most of us use a map or ask for directions. Although you will find many maps to your dreams, the route is yours to choose and follow.

In this chapter you will learn the answers to these questions:

- What are the rules of the road?
- How do you create your personal roadmap?

## What Are the Rules of the Road?

There are seven governing principles which we learned from women who have successfully negotiated the journey and who are now living their dreams (see the summary on the next page). These rules should govern how you proceed at each stage of planning. Even if you do not formalize the planning process, at the very least, these rules should be kept in mind as you make your dreams real.

**Rule 1: Be in the driver's seat.** This is your dream. You need to be in the driver's seat so you can take charge of the route. To take charge means that you will have to make decisions along the way. You have already chosen the dream and now you will choose the direction by selecting from multiple routes, determining the speed, choosing how long to spend on each activity and prioritizing activities. It is you who makes the decisions about the what, where, when and how of your trip.

Sue, who found a career after her youngest child left home, told us: *"One day I woke up and said, 'I'm a teacher. I love teaching. And now I want to teach something that I can teach without having to go back to school.' I realized that I have very good organizational skills and I could easily share*

## THE RULES OF THE ROAD

| | |
|---|---|
| Rule 1 | Be in the driver's seat |
| Rule 2 | Travel light |
| Rule 3 | Check out the multiple routes |
| Rule 4 | Move forward, in any direction |
| Rule 5 | Be alert to danger: Obey the road signs |
| Rule 6 | Don't be a backseat driver |
| Rule 7 | Put your key in the ignition and go |

*them with others who don't. I sat down one night and wrote out ten possible courses that I could teach. I approached a number of institutions and I said, 'This is what I teach. Would you be interested?' I persisted until somebody finally said, 'We would like to try it for a pilot session.'"*

Being in charge does not mean always being in control. There will be many unforeseen events along the way that are beyond your control. There may be some interesting events that pop up that you hadn't anticipated, of which you will want to take advantage. Only if you are in the driver's seat will you be able to respond in a timely way.

The women we interviewed told us how much their lives were shaped by serendipitous events and the unexpected. What characterized these women is that they lived their lives guided by principles and values. When serendipitous events happened, they were well-positioned to respond. They recognized that these new turns in the road would enhance their lives. Remember Gretta who was invited to be chancellor of McGill University. Her education and life's work as a journalist and political activist and her dedication in the university put her in the right place at the right time to be offered and accept the position, even though she had not even applied for it.

**Rule 2: Travel light.** This has two meanings and both are relevant in creating your road map. First, travel light means don't bring too much baggage. Baggage can include your expectations, assumptions, unresolved emotional issues and your history. This is not to say that you should separate yourself from the past. You can't. The past has made you who you are and it carries life's lessons learnt. However, fears, hurts and insecurities can retard or derail writing a new road map. Although you can't leave those parts of yourself at home, you may want to pack them at the bottom of the suitcase.

Remember Blema who became a psychoanalyst. She discovered the importance of divesting baggage before she could create a new road map: *"I was aware that there were certain things that I really wanted to change about myself. I used to say to my husband when we went away on holiday, 'If only I could leave myself at home. I am spoiling my fun by bringing me along.' I decided that I would rationalize my desire to undergo analysis by saying that I was simply looking into it academically and professionally. I began my analysis and I thought, 'This is the most insightful, useful and wonderful thing.' I decided to apply to become an analyst. I would come home and I would say to my teenage children, 'I am so excited. You should hear what I learned today about myself. And if I'm boring you, you just tell me to stop.' So they said 'You're boring us, Mom. We don't want to hear.'"*

The second meaning of travel light is to keep it simple. With simplicity comes a measure of freedom, and with freedom, you can entertain more opportunities. Keeping it simple also helps to guard you from becoming overwhelmed. If you have tried to include too much detail in your road map before you get started, you may never get started. You can build in complexity after you have outlined the basic route.

**Rule 3: Check out multiple routes to your destination.** There are many ways of getting to a dream and no single best route. You need to consider different routes along the way and choose the one that is best suited to you. Don't be daunted if one route doesn't take you where you want to go. There are many ways of getting to a destination. That's what detours are for. In the Vantage Years, because of your life experience, you will know that there are many different ways to achieve your dream. Networking, volunteering and talking to people who are living your dream can help you find those alternative routes. People love to tell you how they got to where they are. Don't be reluctant to ask.

You may be able to move along more quickly if you are familiar with the route or have traveled the road before. Once Linda decided to go into the business of cake designing, she was able to move with surefootedness because of her prior experience in running a small business.

**Rule 4: Move forward, in any direction.** Whether or not you are clear on the route to take, the key is to keep moving. If you stop moving, you'll stall and you'll never reach your destination. Moving forward is about progress, adventure, growth. On the other hand, moving forward takes you into uncharted territory—the unknown, the uncertain, the unpredictable. The tendency may be to stop and shift into reverse because you will feel positive feelings of safety and security. However reverse gear should be reserved only for getting out of a jam. Going back involves retreating, regressing. If you do find yourself in reverse, don't get too comfortable. Comfort can become a rut in which you don't want to get stuck. You can move in any direction as long as you are moving on toward your destination.

Naomi told us how she moved forward. *"After I left my husband I remember sitting in my living room waiting for the ceiling to fall. I had never been on my own. I had two children and he wasn't going to support me. And I just went through it day by day. You do whatever you have in front of you and eventually you get to that place. At the age of forty-five I decided to move to Toronto. All I had was five thousand dollars, no job, simply a great education. I chose to make a turning point. I moved to Toronto. I have never looked back. It was the best decision I ever made."*

**Rule 5: Be alert to danger—obey the road signs**. Any journey is fraught with hurdles, danger signs and bumps in the road. You need to know how to read the signs, understand what they mean, anticipate the danger and react appropriately. Think of some of those warning signals on highways—deer crossings, slippery pavement, steep hills.

How do you recognize a danger signal on your own journey? People who have made the trip before—a friend, a coach, a professional—know which signs to look for, and they can help you. At the same time, beware of seeking counsel from people who see danger lurking at every turn. They may hijack your dreams and stop you in your tracks.

If you realize that you do not have enough money, support, knowledge or skills to get to your destination, look for help. In no case should you lose sight of your destination. Associate with people who can help you achieve your dream by helping you to avoid the dangers and by suggesting alternative routes. You need enablers not naysayers. Remember, your dream must be achieved even if the journey has to be temporarily delayed or rerouted.

Roberta, who looked back on her decision to accept a position in another city, was not alert enough to danger signs: *"After six months, I had to resign from the position because my family didn't want to join me. I could blame my resignation on my husband or my children but it was not their fault. They just said they were not prepared to come within the next year or two and I had to make the most awful decision to leave the work that I loved."*

**Rule 6: Don't be your own backseat driver.** You may have the tendency to second-guess yourself when you are unsure that you're making the best decision. You may see any failure as a failure of your judgment. A single failure is just another stop on the road to success. Treat a failure as an opportunity to start anew. Resist the tendency to abort your dream or to beat up on yourself.

Because you haven't seen this road before, there will be surprise dead ends and many false starts and sputters. When you travel and find yourself at such a juncture, a healthy response is to turn back just enough to find a new route. It isn't to turn back and go home or give up. Notice that Naomi never looked back once she decided to move to Toronto.

**Rule 7: Put your key in the ignition and go.** If you want your dream to become a reality—get started. You may lack confidence initially, but we know of no better recipe for building confidence than to act. It isn't praise that builds confidence, it is competence that builds confidence. Competence comes from doing it. You must at least set a deadline at which to start. And then START.

Renah told us: *"I wanted to get rid of the pennies. I saw the key tags used at gas stations and I saw people counting out their change, the nickels and the pennies, to pay for their coffee at Tim Hortons. I thought, how much time is lost during the transaction of making change? I wanted to do something that was mine. I started up Dexit for small-value transactions to make cash obsolete. I found it easy to persevere even when times were tough because I believed in my dream. I knew someone else would create this business if I didn't, and I didn't want it to be someone else.*" If Renah had not just done it, the idea of a cashless card would have remained an idea.

> **Tip: Beware of analysis paralysis! Thinking and taking time is a means to a goal, not an end in itself. Do not let thinking time change from being a strength to a liability.**

## Exercise: Creating Your Personal Road Map

Creating your road map will show you what you need to do to get you to where you want to go. Once you've started, you have to keep on going, building on what you already have done, reevaluating direction, resetting course. Taking the first step may open up many new possibilities. Having said this, do not forget the Chinese proverb "A journey of a thousand miles starts with a single step." But remember that having taken the first step does not mean you have walked the thousand miles.

In developing the road map to your dream, we recommend you be deliberate and conscious of what you are doing. Remember, you are setting off on a new adventure. You need to formalize the process so that you can be in charge, in the driver's seat (Rule 1). The rules of the road are the governing principles of your plan and should be referred to or kept in mind when completing each activity.

## Activity 1: Identifying Your Destination

Before you get started you have to know where you are going. Reread your dream sheet or do the dream exercises in Chapter 3.

By the end of Chapter 3 you may have defined a firm and specific dream to accomplish, or your dream may have remained vague. During the process of going through the rest of the book, your dream should have become more and more specific. By now you might have found more ways to express your dream. If you've thought of many ideas, you must choose one to work with. Begin with the one that excites you the most.

Going back to Linda's dream, *"I needed to do something creative. Cake design was a natural thing because it combined all the things that I really loved: the sweets, the baking, the decorating and the creative aspect."*

## Activity 2: Answering Questions

Create a set of questions and answers that address the what, where, when, why and how. In this exercise we formalize the questioning activity, an activity that is often informal and taken for granted.

You can take the mystery out of the planning process if you think of planning simply as a series of questions that need answers. You wouldn't think of building a house without a blueprint. Before an architect can create the blueprint, she needs to find out certain information: How large a lot? What type or style of house—bungalow, cottage, etc.? How many rooms? Which direction should the house face? What view? How much to spend? Quality of materials? Time to completion? . . . and so forth. Similarly, before creating your road map you need to ask yourself a series of questions about your dream. The answers that follow will help you plan, as well as give you a new set of more detailed questions to answer.

Laurie knew that if she was going to remain in academia she needed to have a doctorate. At that time, there were no doctoral nursing programs in Canada. Family responsibilities precluded her studying elsewhere. In planning to pursue doctoral studies, she needed answers to the following questions: Would her husband be supportive? How would she combine family and study responsibilities? How would this decision affect her children and family life? What program of study would match her interests and expertise? Who offered such a program? Who would she want to study with? Could she afford to devote the time? How much money would she need? What sources of funding were available? Would she need to work part-time to supplement her income? When should she begin? What type of help did she need at home? . . . Lots of questions, lots of answers, decisions made, route mapped out, dream achieved.

Answering the *what, where, when, why, who* and *how* questions provides the framework for developing the blueprint of your road map. Use these interrogative pronouns to create your own questions around your dream.

At the broadest level, you need to ask yourself, "Why am I doing this?" If you found your authentic dream, your answer is probably, "Because this will achieve my dream." You also need to ask, "What do I hope to get from it?"— satisfaction, money, a day filled with meaningful activities could be some of your answers.

The next question you need to ask is, "What strengths does this dream require?" Go back to the list of strengths that you created in Chapter 5 and single out the ones that are most important to your dream. Look especially at the nine strengths that we suggested are important for dreaming. Write them down. Then ask yourself, "What resources does this dream require?" Go back to Chapter 6 and figure out what resources you will need to realize the dream—health, money, relationships, partners, workers, more education.

Now that you have the answers to these general questions you are ready to ask more specific questions such as

- What obstacles will I face?
- When can I start?
- What do I have to do in a day, a week, a month?
- Will I have to relocate to realize my dream?
- How will I proceed?
- What are my alternate routes?

Take a look at the sample questions to build your road map on pages 218–222. This table outlines sample questions for three different dreams.

### Activity 3: Matching and Mobilizing

Now that you know some of the parameters of your dream, where you are going and what you need to do to get there, sit back and do a reality check.

You have to assess how well your strengths and resources match your dream and what you may need to build on to carry out your plan. Laurie had to match her own strengths (tenacity, pediatric-nursing background, can-do attitude and the right timing) and resources (good health, supportive husband, help with child care and a workable budget and financial aid) to the demands and requirements of the doctoral program.

In Activity 2 you assessed the strengths and resources required for the dream. Refer back to your own strengths and resources which you identified in the exercises in Chapters 5 and 6. Do they match up? How well do they match? What work do you need to do to make them match?

If there is a wide gap between the prerequisites of the dream and your strengths and resources, ask yourself, "Is there a way to close the gap?" You might have to do some retraining or seek others' help to close the gap.

Linda's story continues. Linda looked at what she enjoyed doing and what she was good at. She knew she loved working with her hands, had a well-honed artistic sense, enjoyed making desserts and baking, loved color and design. Her personal style is unique—she loves vintage clothing and folk art. Her cakes are elegant, whimsical and creative. She has designed cakes in the shape of Chanel and Louis Vuitton handbags, Jeeps, Volkswagens and china patterns. Her kitchen was adequate although it needed updating, so she refurbished it after a few years. She had always liked to work but didn't want to work regular hours. She knew she could run a small business. Her prior success had given her that confidence. She had the support of her husband who understood the demands on her time. What she was missing at first was the know-how and a reputation, so she took courses, read books and started off by giving away her cakes as gifts, until her reputation grew.

## Activity 4: Mapping the Route

One of the easiest ways to understand the requirements of your journey is to see it as a series of tasks to be accomplished or action-items. These action-items derive from the answers to the questions you asked and answered in Activity 2 and Activity 3.

- **List your action-items.** For example, when planning a wedding you need to consider such aspects as location, clothes, flowers, food and drink, music, photographer. In addition, you need to estimate the cost involved, the equipment needed, the schedule, the help required. Each choice will require further action.
- **Prioritize your action-items.** Create a detailed plan for each action-item, always keeping your eye on the dream. To identify the action-items for your own dream review Activity 2. Don't hesitate to go back and repeat the activity if you need more detail. Make sure you have considered all the challenges inherent in your dream.
- **Create the schedule and timeline.** Now you are ready to add greater detail, including a schedule and timeline. You may find you want to work step by step towards your dream. Other people find it easier to plan backwards from their goal. If you want to be living your dream in two years, plan backwards and identify the critical points in your path that you need to get done if you are to make this deadline. Working from the dream backwards, in light of all the things you have to do, will tell you how realistic your timeline is.

Linda, the sweater and cake designer, tells how she mapped out the route to deliver her first order of sweaters on time: *"After I designed these four or five little sweaters, I went in to a knitwear boutique and the owner said, 'I'll take X number in children's sizes 2, 4, 6, 8, but I want them in adult sizes as well.' And so I had no choice. I had to make them in big sizes and in little sizes. I walked out of that store and I didn't know what I was going to do. I was terrified and overwhelmed. But I realized I had to do it. When I was in this meeting with the store owner, I was busy writing three of this in this color, four of that, twelve of these, in this size and those sizes. I went in there with great confidence. I didn't let on that I was terrified even before getting the order.*

*"I went to the restaurant across the street and pored over the numbers—seventy sweaters! I thought, 'Oh my God, what am I going to do? I have to get my act together really fast.' I had made a commitment and there were deadlines for delivery. I had lunch. I calmed myself down. Then I designed the path that I had to take. I realized that I would not have time to make all the sweaters myself. The first thing I had to do was to find help. I decided to put ads for knitters in the Italian newspapers. I called the Italian newspapers, gave them the ad in English and they translated it into Italian. I had to interview the women. I had to look at how they knit. I had to write up the instructions. I had to make sure that the sweaters all came out the right size. I started hiring people and looking at their handiwork and supervising them. They knit the pieces for me and I put them all together myself. It was very stressful. But I did it. I took an Italian course so I could talk with my knitters. And that was fun too. It made me feel good because I was able to get the order and because I could finish and deliver it on time."*

If Activity 3 has shown you that you need more training, more help or further education, you need to factor this into your road map—how long the course is, how much it will cost, whether you have the prerequisites or not. Don't be alarmed if it looks as if a lengthy education is the only way to get to where you want to go. Remember Rule 3, there are multiple routes to a goal. You might gain the prerequisite skills by taking a course, doing an internship or getting on-the-job experience.

When Linda embarked on her second interest, cake designing, she describes the additional skills she needed and how she went about getting them. *"I had to learn many, many different techniques in cake decorating. And I didn't know all these techniques when I first started. I knew enough to get started. But along the way I kept teaching myself new techniques and also making up new techniques. At the beginning I went to New York City and I took a one-day wedding-cake course with this famous cake designer. I learned a lot of techniques on that one day. But for the most part, all the other techniques I learned from books. I had to become really familiar with all the different things that you use to decorate a cake. I had to understand what butter cream is, what rolled fondant is, what royal icing is and all the other things that can be used for decorating. But also I had to develop a line of recipes, different flavors and different fillings so that I could offer people great tastes. So I experimented with many different recipes— many different chocolate cakes, many different white cakes until I found a really moist cake and delicious cake that I could vary according to different needs. I also figured out how to do certain things just by looking at pictures and saying, 'Well, how can I do that? How can I make that? Or how can I get that effect?' I'm constantly experimenting.*

*"And I have tons of equipment. I have drawers full of ingredients, brushes and cutters and different kinds of icing tips and things for measuring and different sizes and shapes of pans. I had to accumulate all this stuff in order to be able to do all these designs. I'm always looking for new things. At this point I have just about everything there is to have."*

Linda could have taken a year-long cake-designing course at college, but instead she customized her education to meet the requirements of her dream. That way, she was already starting on her way to living her dream.

> **Tip: It is important to create a schedule and to fill each day with actions, big or small, that will move you towards living your dream. When you hit a bump in the road, you then can feel confident because you have routines, plans and activities scheduled. In a way, mapping the route can make you feel as though you are living your dream already.**

### Activity 5: Making the Decision

Put a stake in the ground, decide what you will do and stick to your plan.

Even though you may not have planned all the action-items that make up your road map, you have to move forward, at least on some. Now is the time to be governed by Rule 7: Put your key in the ignition and go. Setting a date somewhat in advance, gearing up for that launch date and honoring that launch date is a good way to keep moving.

You have to be flexible and realistic. You may have to modify the launch date because of extenuating circumstances or because you may not have considered some essential elements. You may decide to wait. Just be sure you're delaying for the right reasons, not because of fear or paralysis.

**Activity 6: Moving Forward—Getting into the Vicinity.**
Being in the vicinity means getting as close to your dream as you possibly can. It gives you first-hand exposure and knowledge of how your dreams can work. If your dream is to be in the film industry, you may find ways to get in through screenwriting, set design, editing, producing or developing. You may get into the vicinity by working in the industry, volunteering in the industry or meeting people who work in the industry. Networking is critical to getting into the vicinity.

Linda began her cake-design business slowly. *"I started giving the cakes away just as gifts. I tried to make them as fabulous as I could so that people would say, 'Oh my God, that's terrific.' And then people would be interested because it was a new art form and they hadn't seen anything like that before. When I first started making wedding cakes, a friend of mine was doing a table setting for a fund-raising event. She asked me if I wanted to do the table with her. I said 'Sure.' We decided on a wedding-table theme and that the centerpiece would be a wedding cake. I did the wedding cake for that table. I remember I had no business cards at the time and people kept asking me for my card. I stood there the entire time writing my name and phone number and handing it out to people. So that's how it happened at the beginning."*

### Activity 7: Modifying the Road Map and Creating a Plan B.

Know that at some point you might have to make changes—minor or major. Be prepared to modify the plan or create an alternate plan to deal with the unexpected.

You need to consider contingencies and "What if" scenarios to be in the driver's seat (Rule 1). What if someone else has the same idea and gets there first? What if I don't get into the course I need? What if my financial support falls away? What if my partner falls ill or changes his/her mind? What are my other options? Do I have to find another dream or can I change course, pick another route?

Never lose sight of your dream. Don't abort your dream. Find another way to get there (Rule 3). It might turn out even better. In taking a detour, you may stumble across new avenues that you had never noticed, new ways of doing things and new people to do them with. Be flexible because the opportunity might present in a different form than what you had expected.

Those who have taken the time to match, map and mobilize, and make the decisions, have the confidence and flexibility to change course. These activities should give you the ability to recognize an opportunity and to seize the initiative. You are more likely to be alert to early warning signs (Rule 5) and not to second-guess yourself (Rule 6) when a change of course is indicated.

> **Tip:** Be flexible enough in your plans that you can respond to the unexpected and take advantage of opportunities to improvise.

Linda created her Plan B when she agreed to knit adult sweaters along with children's sweaters. If she hadn't made that decision—if she had told the store owner that she didn't make adult sweaters—she would never have had the chance to design sweaters for the world's First Ladies.

You are closer to your dream. The rules of the road are now fixed in your mind, and you have begun or even completed the planning exercise. You already have started on your dream. Congratulations!

In the next chapter, we outline a number of signposts that are indicators that you are living your dream. One of the signposts for Linda was when she said: *"I love this so much. I wish I had found this ten years earlier."*

| | | SAMPLE QUESTIONS TO BUILD YOUR ROAD MAP | | |
|---|---|---|---|---|
| Guiding Questions | Sample Dream | Sample Dream | Sample Dream | |
| | Planning a trip | Creating a garden | Providing a retreat for women by owning and running an inn | |
| Why am I doing this? | • Do I need a change, or just a rest? | • Why do I want to create a garden? Do I love flowers or do I just need a place for myself? | • Is this the best way for me to achieve my goal of helping women? | |
| What do I need to consider? | • Where am I going?<br>• When am I going?<br>• How long will I be there?<br>• How long will it take to get there?<br>• How much will it cost?<br>• How much time do I have?<br>• What do I want to see along the way?<br>• What is the weather like?<br>• Where am I going to stay?<br>• Who is coming with me?<br>• Do I want to swim, scuba, sightsee, visit relatives? | • What kind of garden?<br>• What kind of flowers?<br>• Perennials or annuals?<br>• What flowers grow in our climate?<br>• Where do I get help? Advice? Where do I buy the different plants?<br>• What part of my garden is sunny? Shady?<br>• When can I start planting?<br>• What colors do I like?<br>• How large a garden?<br>• How much will it cost? | • What type of retreat? Spa? Meditation center? Learning resource center?<br>• When are prime seasons?<br>• Who is the market? Age of women, group of women?<br>• Where would I like it to be located?<br>• How much will it cost?<br>• How much can I afford?<br>• How large an inn?<br>• How do I market this concept?<br>• Will this be a full-time job? | |

| SAMPLE QUESTIONS TO BUILD YOUR ROAD MAP | | | |
|---|---|---|---|
| Guiding Questions | Sample Dream | Sample Dream | Sample Dream |
| | Planning a trip | Creating a garden | Providing a retreat for women by owning and running an inn |
| | | • How long is the season?<br>• How much time do I have?<br>• Do I need a landscape architect? | • How will I make money in the start-up years?<br>• Who can help me? |
| What strengths does the dream need? | • Am I energetic and tenacious enough?<br>• Can I navigate with confidence?<br>• Can I plan and problem solve well enough?<br>• Am I resilient and resourceful?<br>• Can I make this happen and smile? | • Am I enthusiastic and creative enough?<br>• Do I have enough imagination?<br>• Am I optimistic that I'll have the staying power to last the season?<br>• Do I like being alone in the garden for hours?<br>• Am I a good organizer and planner? | • Am I ambitious and tenacious enough?<br>• Am I sociable enough and do I like people enough to serve my customers?<br>• Do I have the specific skills required: cooking, gardening, maintenance, etc.?<br>• Am I compassionate enough to listen to my customers' problems? and easy-going enough not to take them on as my own? |

## SAMPLE QUESTIONS TO BUILD YOUR ROAD MAP

| Guiding Questions | Sample Dream<br>Planning a trip | Sample Dream<br>Creating a garden | Sample Dream<br>Providing a retreat for women by owning and running an inn |
|---|---|---|---|
| What resources does the dream require? | • Am I healthy, strong enough?<br>• Do I have enough money?<br>• Do I need a companion or friend? Who should I go with?<br>• Can I read a map?<br>• Do I have enough time?<br>• Did I do my homework? | • Am I healthy, strong and flexible enough?<br>• Do I have enough money?<br>• Do I need any help? A coach? A gardener?<br>• Do I have the time?<br>• Did I do my homework? | • Do I have the emotional and physical stamina?<br>• Do I have enough money?<br>• Do I need a partner? Type of help?<br>• Do I have the support of my family?<br>• Do I have the time? |
| What are the possible obstacles and fears? | • Do I want to travel alone? If not, why not?<br>• How will I find places to stay? Eat?<br>• How dangerous is it? How will I protect myself? | • What happens if I choose the wrong plants?<br>• Who will tend the garden when I am away? | • Do I have the experience to do this?<br>• What if the market is crowded?<br>• How will I know when to give up? |

## SAMPLE QUESTIONS TO BUILD YOUR ROAD MAP

| Guiding Questions | Sample Dream: Planning a trip | Sample Dream: Creating a garden | Sample Dream: Providing a retreat for women by owning and running an inn |
|---|---|---|---|
| | • How will I find my way? How will I navigate while I am driving?<br>• Is it too long? Will I get bored? | • How do I know where to plant? What to plant? When to plant?<br>• Will my garden grow (be successful)? | • What risks are involved? Is it too risky an adventure for my comfort zone?<br>• What if nobody comes?<br>• What happens if I can't get the skilled help to make it a retreat?<br>• What happens if I can't find the right suppliers? |
| Am I ready? | • What will it take for me to go on the trip?<br>• How much do I want this?<br>• What steps have I taken?<br>• Have I completed all the preparations? Contact numbers? Hotel bookings? Mail stop? Newspaper? Immunizations and so on? | • What will it take for me to start my garden?<br>• How much do I want this?<br>• What steps have I taken?<br>• Have I completed all the preparations? Plans, plants, soil, fertilizer, gardening tools? | • What will it take for me to start my inn?<br>• How much do I want this?<br>• What steps have I taken?<br>• Have I completed all the preparations? Inn built, financing in place, staff hired, equipment bought, rooms furnished? |

## SAMPLE QUESTIONS TO BUILD YOUR ROAD MAP

| Guiding Questions | Sample Dream: Planning a trip | Sample Dream: Creating a garden | Sample Dream: Providing a retreat for women by owning and running an inn |
|---|---|---|---|
| When can I start? | • Do I have what I need to get started? (e.g., money, time, friend) <br> • Do I have a departure and return date? | • How long will the preparations take? <br> • When can I set a start date? <br> • Do I have to wait until the spring? | • How long will the preparations take? <br> • When should I submit my business plan? <br> • What should my opening date be? |
| How can I build in contingency plans? | • What if . . . it rains? Car breaks down? I get sick? | • What if . . . infestation of insects and animals? I can't get the seeds, bulbs, flowers? My plants die? | • What if . . . I can't find a site, an inn? I can't get financing? I can't get staff? <br> • What if . . . customers don't come or there is not a need for this type of inn? How will I know? <br> • What is my next best choice? |
| What do I have to do, in a month, a week, a day? | • What's the last date possible for booking my ticket? <br> • Do I have to request time off work? | • If I want annuals, when do I plant them? <br> • When do I have to order bulbs and other supplies? <br> • Do I have to care for the garden every day? | • When do I need my financing in place? <br> • What do I have to do now to fill the inn in the summer? |

ten

# SIGNPOSTS: ON YOUR WAY TO LIVING YOUR DREAM

*I dread success. To have succeeded is to have finished one's business on earth, like the male spider who is killed by the female the moment he has succeeded in his courtship. I like a state of continual becoming, with a goal in front and not behind.*

— GEORGE BERNARD SHAW

THE LITMUS TEST of whether you are living your dream is how you feel about yourself and your life. Your authentic dream should make you feel the way you want to feel about yourself and should help you live the life you have designed for yourself. This is because your dream resonates with your values and gives your life purpose and direction.

The chapter begins with an exercise: How Do I Know This is My Dream? The exercise gives you a list of questions to answer to help you determine whether the dream you are pursuing still fits. It should remind you of Chapter 2—Why You Need to Have Dreams.

But you also need to be alert to feelings and behaviors that show that you are veering off course. They, too, are oulined in this chapter.

Finally, this chapter shows you the signposts that you are living your dream. These signposts tell you the extent to which you are moving towards living the life you designed. Although Signposts is the last chapter in this book, you may already have been taking some of these "temperature checks" along the way.

---

## Exercise: How Do I Know This Is My Dream?
(Time to complete: 10 minutes)

We have compiled a list of questions (opposite page) that you can use to further evaluate whether this is the dream you want to be pursuing. Once you've put the key in the ignition you can answer the questions in the exercise at any stage in the process. You should try to do this exercise at set times: three months, six months and a year after you have started on your dream.

As you move towards fulfilling your dream, you may experience doubts, worries and concerns. However, if the dream still excites you to the point where it sustains you and drives you forward, or at least helps you stay the course, then it is your authentic dream.

Keep in mind that your dream will continue to evolve as you evolve. It may take many different forms, some of which you had imagined and many more that will bring wonder and surprise. As Nicole told us: *"You dream of one little thing and it becomes something else. That's how dreams evolve."*

## HOW DO I KNOW THIS IS MY DREAM?

| | Yes | No |
|---|---|---|
| Does my dream feel right for me? | | |
| Do I still feel passionate about my dream? | | |
| Am I animated when I talk about my dream? | | |
| Am I focused and not easily distracted when working at my dream? | | |
| Am I working hard at my dream? | | |
| Am I prepared to make sacrifices to achieve my dream? | | |
| Am I proud to talk about my dream? | | |
| Even though I feel stress, is the dream worth pursuing? | | |
| Does my dream give my life direction? | | |
| Do I feel energized? | | |
| Can I see myself inside the dream? | | |
| Does my dream make me smile? | | |

## How Do I Know If I Am Veering Off Course?

Watch for the following feelings and behaviors that show you that you might be veering off course:

- loss of self-confidence
- feeling at a standstill
- avoiding people
- feeling anxious
- dwelling on bodily complaints
- loss of sleep
- dwelling on past achievements
- feeling frustrated
- feeling stuck and paralyzed
- dreading the future

If you find yourself identifying with some of these feelings and behaviors, first ask yourself if they are related to your dream or if they are caused by other factors. If your feelings are related to the dream, you may want to revisit your dream. If these feelings and behaviors are not connected to your dream, you may have to deal with those concerns by seeking help before continuing with your dream. If you suffer from depression or are experiencing family problems, you will need to address those issues before you can concentrate on your dream. Though, working on your dream may help you get over this bump in the road.

> **Tip:** Sometimes dreaming can be a pleasant diversion from your problems or it can even be a solution. Sometimes, though, it can be an extra source of stress. Know the difference and act accordingly.

## What Are the Signposts That You Are Living Your Dream?

You are living your dream, or at the very least on the right path, if you can identify with at least three of the seven signposts listed in the table on the next page: Signposts On My Way to Living My Dream. It is important to take time to assess or at least reflect on where you are. Some of you may ignore, minimize or gloss over your achievements, unaware of how much progress you have made or of how far you have come in living a meaningful life. As women we often tend to underestimate ourselves.

**Signpost 1: Sense of balance.** When your life feels more in sync, more in balance, you are living your dream. You feel that you have achieved better balance among the different facets of your life—work, friends, family, time for yourself. This engenders a greater sense of contentment. You feel that what you are doing is a better reflection of who you are. You feel that how you are living and the choices you have made are more in tune with your passions. You feel more energized and hopeful. This is not to say that you have to feel happy all the time. But you experience fewer moments of self-doubt and more moments of harmony and joy.

Melanie, at thirty-nine, decided, *"I'm going to train as a couples and family therapist. It's something very important to*

## SIGNPOSTS ON MY WAY TO LIVING MY DREAM

| | |
|---|---|
| Signpost 1 | Sense of balance |
| Signpost 2 | Comfortable with change |
| Signpost 3 | Comfortable with who you are |
| Signpost 4 | Sense of contribution |
| Signpost 5 | Life is an adventure |
| Signpost 6 | Not yearning for the past |
| Signpost 7 | In charge |

*me. I'm going to do it now. And I started to train with full-time work, young kids and the whole bit. So at forty-eight I have almost completed my training. I know this was a turning point for me. It was a good one because it feels very right and I'm very passionate about it."*

Not only are you aware of the change in yourself but others also begin to notice and comment on how well you look and how happy you seem. Susan told us: *"I left banking and worked for nine months in a scuba store. People just sort of said, 'Oh great, are you happy?' Then, after many more changes, my husband and I made a bold move to the country. Our daughter, interestingly enough, keeps saying, 'I've never heard you two happier.'"*

**Signpost 2: Comfortable with change.** When you see change as a challenge and no longer dread it or feel apprehensive, you are on the right path. You may even welcome the new forks in the road. Gwen, recalling changes, said: *"Making the decision to leave my first job was difficult for many reasons. But the second time was not that difficult. The first change is the hardest. It went well and this encouraged me to change again. Once you've made a couple of changes and they have worked out, another one isn't such a big deal."*

**Signpost 3: Comfortable with who you are.** When you are not spending as much time trying to "find yourself," you are on the path to living your dream. When you care more about what you have accomplished and what you are doing and are less preoccupied with what you have not done or have not yet accomplished, you are living your dream. Faith told us: *"I am bored with the question about who I am."* Heather echoed these sentiments: *"The best thing that happened to me between forty-five and fifty was that I stopped focusing on myself."* Barbara told us: *"If I won the million-dollar lottery, I wouldn't change my life much."* You will experience a level of comfort that you may not have previously experienced—a real acceptance of yourself. Patricia Gray, the founder of the Canadian Animal Distress Network, described this signpost clearly when she said: "The feeling that says, 'Hey, I am who I am; I like who I am; and I am content to be who I am.'"[1]

**Signpost 4: Sense of contribution.** When you feel that you are making a valuable contribution and are making a difference in your life and in the lives of others, you are living your dream. Dianne asks herself a series of questions to determine that she is living the life she wants to be living: *"For me it is about quality of life. About savoring life and being responsible—not taking life for granted. What is my epitaph? What will it say on my tombstone? Am I actually moving towards that? It is also a question of values. What are my values? What is my contribution to society?"* If your answers to questions such as these satisfy you, then you are definitely living your dream.

**Signpost 5: Life is an adventure.** When you experience life as fun and as an adventure, you are living your dream. Some of you may even welcome life's unpredictability, tolerate its uncertainties and "go with the flow." You live and enjoy the present, while at the same time anticipating the future. In fact, you are excited about moving on. This state is a good indicator that you are doing what you like and like what you are doing. For Ann it is *"just being very open to things that intrigue me."*

**Signpost 6: Not yearning for the past.** When you can celebrate and be proud of past achievements, and at the same time have no desire to go back to the good old days, you are living your dream. Naomi told us: *"Surprisingly, most people ask, 'Don't you miss it?' There were all these nice perks.*

*I was picked up every morning with a limousine and brought to work and taken home. There were TV cameras around all the time. When I retired, I went from being a known person to being anonymous. I like being anonymous. I can walk down the street in my jeans, my hair not done, no lipstick. No, I don't miss it."*

Pat figured out that she didn't want what she had thought she wanted. *"I saw an ad in the job column that I applied for recently. Though I applied, I didn't really want it. What a relief when I wasn't called for an interview. I guess I was testing the waters but I know now that I really didn't want to go back into the world of work. I think it would have taken a very remarkable job to get me back into the work world again. I think that's what's unique about being at this stage of our life. We know what we don't want and I don't want to go back to work full-time."*

**Signpost 7: Being in charge.** When you are finally marching to the beat of your own drum and have taken charge of your life, you are on the right path, or living your dream. As Viktor Frankl, the philosopher, said, "The last of human freedoms is to choose one's attitude in any given set of circumstances."[2] Living your dream takes you steps beyond just choosing your attitude. It takes you to a whole new level in making choices that firmly place you in the driver's seat of your life. You feel that your life is in balance, in harmony. You do not continuously feel pulled, stretched and overextended. That's the reward of having taken charge and being in charge.

When you feel that all these signposts reflect your life, you'll know you've transitioned through the Vantage Process and are finally at Phase 5—Living the Dream.

## Parting Words

Our aim in writing this book has been to create a new vantage point for women to benefit from the many possibilities that arrive at this time of life. The Vantage Years are those years in which you begin to reap the rewards of experience and wisdom, and take full advantage of your strengths and resources.

We have shared with you what we have learned over the course of our own lives, what we have learned from each other, from our work and what we have learned from the many women with whom we have talked. The women to whom we talked were at different ages, came from different backgrounds, life circumstances and countries. They had different values, lifestyles and work histories. They were homemakers, nurses, businesspeople, office administrators, entrepreneurs, lawyers, physicians, educators, psychologists. They took pleasure in family and friends. They enjoyed writing, cooking, gardening, traveling, working, reading, decorating, music, painting, shopping and just hanging out. They were involved in learning, volunteering and community services. They shared their challenges, their wins, their losses and struggles, their triumphs and disappointments and their hopes for the future. They all recognized that the Vantage Years would be a significant phase of their life and that they needed to make these years count.

We learned that the Vantage Years are the time to examine your life script, to edit out those "should haves," "could haves" and "would haves" and replace them with "can dos."

We learned the importance of exploring the positives and possibilities in every event rather than the negatives and impossibilities.

We learned the importance of broadening the realm of possibilities by creating options, forging new pathways and making choices that fit.

We learned the importance of taking charge of our lives.

We learned the importance of time—taking time, making time and using this time for dreaming.

We learned that no act or dream is too small. Even the smallest act can make the most profound difference to the quality of your life.

But above all, we learned the importance of having dreams, getting in touch with your dreams and living your dreams.

# PERMISSIONS

The authors are grateful to the following for permission to reprint from previously published material. Every effort has been made to contact the copyright holders; in the event of an inadvertent omission or error, please notify the publisher.

From *New Passages* by Gail Sheehy (New York: Random House, 1995).

From *Alice's Adventures in Wonderland & Through the Looking Glass* by Lewis Carroll (New York; Toronto: Alfred A. Knopf, 1992), 76.

From *Revising Herself: The Story of Women's Identity from College to Midlife* by Ruthellen Josselson (New York: Oxford University Press, 1996), 9.

From *Wisdom for the Way* by Charles Swindoll. Copyright 2001 by Charles Swindoll. Used by permission of J. Countryman, a division of Thomas Nelson, Inc.

From *The Quotable Businesswoman: Observations on Business and Life from Women at the Top* by Laura Boswell (Kansas City: Andrews McMeel, 2001), 74.

From *Two Old Women* by Velma Wallis (Seattle: Epicenter Press, 1993).

From *Hard Won Wisdom* by Fawn Germer (New York: Perigee, 2001), 256.

From *Women Confronting Retirement: A Nontraditional Guide* by Nan Bauer-Maglin and Alice Radosh, eds. (New Brunswick, NJ; London: Rutgers Univ. Press, 2003), 5.

From *Madam Secretary: A Memoir* by Madeleine Albright. Copyright © 2003 Madeleine Albright. Reprinted by permission of Hyperion, 512.

From *The Complete Idiot's Guide to Change Management* by Jeff Davidson (Indianapolis: Alpha Books, 2002), 51.

From *World Enough and Time: Conversations with Canadian Women at Midlife* by Andrea Mudry (Toronto: Dundurn Press, 1996), 62.

From *Man's Search for Meaning: An Introduction to Logotherapy* by Viktor E. Frankl (New York: Beacon Press, 1984), 9.

# ENDNOTES

## 1: Dreams and the Vantage Years

1. Sheehy, G., *New Passages* (New York: Random House, 1995).

2. Lackman, M.E. and J.B. James, "Charting the Course of Midlife Development: An Overview," in *Multiple Paths of Midlife Development,* M.E. Lackman and J.B. James, eds. (Chicago: Univ. Chic. Press, 1997), 1–17.

3. Elder, G.H., "Human Lives in Changing Societies: Life Course Developmental Insights," in *Developmental Science,* R.B. Cairns, G.H. Elder, and E.J. Costello, eds. (Cambridge: Cambridge University Press, 1996), 45–61.

4. Levinson, D.J., *The Seasons of a Woman's Life* (New York: Alfred A. Knopf, 1996).

## 2: Why You Need to Have Dreams

1. Carroll, L., *Alice's Adventures in Wonderland & Through the Looking Glass* (New York; Toronto: Alfred A. Knopf, 1992), 76.

2. Emmons, R.A., "Striving and Feeling," in *The Psychology of Action: Linking Cognition and Motivation to Behavior,* P.M. Gollwitzer and J.A. Bargh, eds. (New York: Guilford Press, 1996), 313–37.

## 3: Getting in Touch with Your Dreams

1. Tripp, R.T., *The International Thesaurus of Quotations* (Great Britain: Penguin, 1976), 264.

2. Schmuck, P. and K.M. Sheldon, "Life Goals and Well-Being: To the Frontiers of Life Goal Research," in *Life Goals and Well-Being: Towards a Positive Psychology of Human Striving,* P. Schmuck and K.M. Sheldon, eds. (Seattle: Hogrefe & Huber, 2001), 1–17.

## 4: The Vantage Process: Where Are You?

1. Mercer, R.T., E.G. Nichols, and G.C. Doyle, *Transitions in a Woman's Life: Major Life Events in Developmental Context* (New York: Springer Publishing Company, 1989), 2.

2. Mishel, M.H., "Reconceptualization of Uncertainty in Illness." *Image: Journal of Nursing Scholarship*, 22 (1990): 256–62.

3. Jacobs, R.D., *The Way In: Journal Writing for Self-Discovery* (New York: Stewart, Tabori & Chang, 2001).

4. Josselson, R., *Revising Herself: The Story of Women's Identity from College to Midlife* (New York: Oxford University Press, 1996), 9.

5. Mintzberg, H., *The Nature of Managerial Work* (Englewood Cliffs, NJ: Prentice-Hall, 1980).

6. Swindoll, C.R., *Wisdom for the Way* (Nashville: J. Countryman, 2001).

7. Reivich, K. and J. Gillham, "Learned Optimism: The Measurement of Explanatory Style," in *Positive Psychological Assessment: A Handbook of Models and Measures*, S.J. Lopez and C.R. Snyder, eds. (Washington, D.C.: American Psychological Assn., 2003), 57–74.

## 5: Strengths: Your Best Investment Is You

1. Wallis, V., *Two Old Women* (Seattle: Epicenter Press, 1993).

2. Rubin, H., *The Princessa: Machiavelli for Women* (New York: Dell, 1998).

3. Boswell, L., *The Quotable Businesswoman: Observations on Business and Life from Women at the Top* (Kansas City: Andrews McMeel, 2001), 74.

4. Buckingham, M. and Clifton, D.O., *Now, Discover Your Strengths* (New York: Simon & Schuster, 2001) quoted in Foreword by D. Clifton in Lopez, S.J. and C.R. Snyder, eds. *Positive Psychological Assessment: A Handbook of Models and Measures* (Washington, D.C.: American Psychological Assn, 2003), xiii.

5. Thomas, S.P., "Psychosocial Correlates of Women's Self-Related Physical/Social Health in Middle Adulthood," in *Multiple Paths of Midlife Development*, M.E. Lackman and J.B. James, eds. (Chicago: Univ. Chic. Press, 1997), 257–91.

6. Seligman, M.E.P., "Positive Psychology, Positive Prevention and Positive Therapy," in *Handbook of Positive Psychology*, C.R. Snyder and S.J. Lopez, eds. (New York: Oxford Publishing Press, 2002), 3–12.

7. Germer, F., *Hard Won Wisdom* (New York: Perigee, 2001), 256.

8. Bandura, A., *Self-Efficacy: The Exercise of Control* (New York: W.H. Freeman, 1997).

9. Chess, S. and A. Thomas, *Goodness of Fit: Clinical Applications From Infancy Through Adult Life* (Philadelphia: Brunner/Mazel, 1999).

10. Goleman, D., *Emotional Intelligence* (New York: Bantam Books, 1995).

11. Goleman, D., *Working with Emotional Intelligence* (New York: Bantam Books, 1998).

## 6: Resources: Taking Stock and Taking Charge

1. Thomas, S.P., "Psychosocial Correlates of Women's Self-Related Physical/Social Health in Middle Adulthood," in *Multiple Paths of Midlife Development*, M.E. Lackman and J.B. James, eds. (Chicago: Univ. Chic. Press, 1997), 257–91.

2. Spiro III, A., "Health in Mid-Life: Toward a Life-Span View," in *Handbook for Midlife Development*, M.E. Lachman, ed. (New York: John Wiley & Sons, 2001), 156–87.

3. 50connect.co.UK, "KIPPERS Eating Your Retirement Fund," http://www.50connect.co.uk/50c/articlepages/finance_index.asp?sc=pensions&aID=9078, 2004.

4. Bender, C.B., *Don't Squat with Your Spurs On: A Cowboy's Guide to Life* (Layton, UT: Gibbs Smith, 1992), 93.

5. Montana, G., *Never Ask a Man the Size of His Spread: A Cowgirl's Guide to Life* (Layton, UT: Gibbs Smith, 1995), 39.

## 7: Myths: The Hijackers of Dreams

1. Ward, R.A. and G. Spitze, "Sandwiched Marriages: The Implications of Child and Parent Relations for Marital Quality in Midlife." *Social Forces*, 77 (2) (1998): 647–66.

2. Hunter, S. and M. Sundel, "Introduction: An Examination of Key Issues Concerning Midlife," in *Midlife Myths: Issues, Findings, and Practice Implications,* S. Hunter and M. Sundel, eds. (Newbury Park: Sage, 1989), 8–29.

3. Kuhn, D., *Does Memory Development Belong on an Endangered Topic List?* Child Development, 2000. 71: p. 21–25.

4. McEvoy, G.M. and W.F. Cascio, "Cumulative Evidence of the Relationship Between Employee Age and Job Performance," *Journal of Applied Psychology,* Vol. 74 #1 (1989): 11–17.

5. Baltes, P.B. and M.M. Baltes, "Psychological Perspectives on Successful Aging: The Model of Selective Optimization with Compensation," in *Successful Aging: Perspectives from the Behavioral Sciences,* P.B. Baltes and M.M. Baltes, eds. (New York: Cambridge Press, 1990), 1–34.

6. Holmes, T.H. and R.H. Rahe, "The Social Readjustment Scale," *Journal of Psychosomatic Research,* 11, (1967): 213–18.

7. Bauer-Maglin, N. and A. Radosh, eds. *Women Confronting Retirement: A Nontraditional Guide* (New Brunswick, NJ: London: Rutgers Univ. Press, 2003), 5.

8. Lapierre, S. et al., "Aspirations and Well-Being in Old Age," in *Life Goals and Well-Being: Towards a Positive Psychology of Human Striving,* P. Schmuck and K.M. Sheldon, eds. (Seattle: Hogrefe & Huber, 2001), 102–15.

9. Albright, M., *Madam Secretary: A Memoir* (New York: Hyperion, 2003), 512.

10. McAdams, D.P., "Generativity in Midlife," in *Handbook for Midlife Development,* M.E. Lachman, ed. (New York: John Wiley & Sons, 2001), 395–443.

11. MacDermid, S.M., G. Heilbrun, and L.G. DeHaan, "The Generativity of Employed Mothers in Multiple Roles: 1979 and 1991," in *Multiple Paths of Midlife Development,* M.E. Lackman and J.B. James, eds. (Chicago: Univ. Chic. Press, 1997), 207–39.

12. *Age Discrimination in Employment Amendments of 1986,* Pub Law 592, 100 Stat. 3342, October 31, 1986.

13. Greer, G., *The Change: Women, Aging and Menopause* (New York: Ballantine Books, 1993).

## 8: Readiness: If Not Now, When?

1. Stein, J., ed. *Random House Dictionary* (New York: Ballantine Books, 1980), 730.

2. Dalton, C.C. and L.N. Gottlieb, "The Concept of Readiness to Change," *Journal of Advanced Nursing*, 42 (2) (2003): 1–10.

3. Miller, W.R. and S. Rollnick, *Motivational Interviewing: Preparing People for Change*, 2nd ed. (New York: Guilford Press, 2002), 16.

4. Davidson, J., *The Complete Idiot's Guide to Change Management* (Indianapolis: Alpha Books, 2002), 51.

## 10: Signposts: On Your Way to Living Your Dream

1. Mudry, A., *World Enough and Time: Conversations with Canadian Women at Midlife* (Toronto: Dundurn Press, 1996), 62.

2. Frankl, V.E., *Man's Search for Meaning: An Introduction to Logotherapy* (New York: Beacon Press, 1984), 9.

# ACKNOWLEDGMENTS

This book has been a joy to write. We wrote on a topic about which we both felt passionate and learned much about ourselves, each other, other women's experiences and the challenges and rewards of these middle years. We met many wonderful people to whom we are deeply indebted.

A very special thanks to Arielle Gottlieb, our first fan, who encouraged us to move forward. We thank Robert Vineberg and Michael Levine who recognized the potential of the project and introduced us to Bruce Westwood. Bruce Westwood and Natasha Daneman, our agents, have been in our corner and guided us along this new and unfamiliar road. Bruce knew that Anne Collins, Publisher of Random House Canada, was the right person for this project. It has been a joy to work with Anne and her team at Random House. Kendall Anderson has been the editor par excellence. She immediately "got it" and has been a very vocal champion. Anne and Kendall's excellent suggestions and insights have strengthened this book considerably. We are also very grateful to the team at Random House for all their work.

We are indebted to Joanna Toti and Jill Martis, our terrific research team who were involved with all aspects of this book. We appreciate the sage counsel of Earl Heiber and Stephen Roth.

We had great readers, whose comments on the proposal and subsequent drafts of the book were invaluable, especially Linda Switkin (our most enthusiastic fan) and Adrienne Rosenswig, who devoted so much time and gave their whole hearts to this book. We thank Oren Katz for his enthusiasm and for translating our ideas into graphic representation. We appreciate the research help on specific topics we got from Jason Rosenswig, Rosemarie Scissons and Howard Richler. A special thanks to Sandra Heitner for her work with the focus group and to Ruth Getter, who read the final draft so diligently.

Our profound gratitude goes to the many women who shared their stories with us. Their candor, honesty and spiritedness gave us new insights into these Vantage Years. They serve as models with whom many women will identify.

Laurie: Family has always been a great source of strength, love and support. To my wonderful children, from whom I derive my zest for life and my energy: Michah, and his wife, Ilana, and Arielle. I thank Mary Richler and Judith Fellner. I am grateful to Linda Switkin, Jonathan Richler and Lenore Frohman, most enthusiastic mavens. I am blessed with wonderful nieces and a nephew—Peter Gottlieb, a loyal and excited supporter. My niece, Tamar Fellner, was excited about this project and her untimely death makes the completion of this book even more poignant.

The real joy in this book has been working with Deanna. Ever since we first met, I have admired her, respected her and held her in awe. I am even more in awe of her now and feel privileged to be the beneficiary of her generosity, fun-loving spirit, intelligence, graciousness and wisdom. My final words of gratitude are reserved for my husband and soulmate, Bruce, whose boundless and unflagging love, gentleness and encouragement have given my life its meaning and who has enabled us to live our dreams.

Deanna: I am grateful to my sister Avra Schactman, who took such pride in this achievement. To my mother, Lottie Schactman, a role model, who always encouraged me with admiration and warm smiling eyes. To my late father, who taught me how to love and live with humor. To Jason, Adrienne and Oren for always being in my corner. To my extended family of uncles, aunts, cousins, and friends, who told their stories, gave me the thumbs-up and publicized this book. To everyone who has touched my life in big and small ways so that I can learn the rules of the road and revel in these Vantage Years. To Laurie, my co-author, best friend, kindred spirit: I respect, love and admire you more each day as I get to know you better and better. You made my dream come true. To my husband, Michael, my *bashert,* my love, my confidant and biggest booster—my heart is yours.

# NOTES

# NOTES

# NOTES

# NOTES

LAURIE GOTTLIEB and DEANNA ROSENSWIG are boomers facing retirement. They are wives and mothers, and have been friends since high school.

LAURIE GOTTLIEB holds an M.Sc. in nursing and a Ph.D. in developmental psychology. She is a professor and holds the Flora Madeline Shaw Chair of Nursing at McGill University. She is the editor of *CJNR*—an international nursing research journal. She lives in Montreal.

DEANNA ROSENSWIG holds a B.Com. and an M.B.A. She rose to the highest echelons of banking as an Executive Vice President of the Bank of Montreal and has been a career commercial and corporate banker. Deanna is a director and trustee on the boards of corporate and not-for-profit organizations and has a special interest in small business and micro-finance for women. She lives in Toronto.